Exodus
Part Two

Exodus
Part Two

Exodus 16–40

Stephen J. Binz

with Little Rock Scripture Study staff

LITURGICAL PRESS
Collegeville, Minnesota

www.littlerockscripture.org

Cover design by Ann Blattner. Interior art by Ned Bustard. Images on pages 49, 50, and 56 courtesy of
Getty Images. Map on page 95 created by Robert Cronan of Lucidity Information Design, LLC.

This symbol indicates material that was created by Little Rock Scripture Study to supplement the
biblical text and commentary. Some of these inserts first appeared in the *Little Rock Catholic Study
Bible*; others were created specifically for this book by Amy Ekeh.

1   2   3   4   5   6   7   8   9

Library of Congress Cataloging-in-Publication Data

Names: Binz, Stephen J., 1955– author.
Title: Exodus / Stephen J. Binz with Little Rock Scripture Study staff.
Description: Collegeville : Liturgical Press, 2019– | Series: Little Rock Scripture Study.
Identifiers: LCCN 2019001482 (print) | LCCN 2019009043 (ebook) | ISBN 9780814664766 (eBook) |
    ISBN 9780814664520 (pbk.)
Subjects: LCSH: Bible. Exodus—Textbooks.
Classification: LCC BS1245.55 (ebook) | LCC BS1245.55 .B56 2019 (print) | DDC 222/.120071—dc23
LC record available at https://lccn.loc.gov/2019001482

Exodus, Part One: ISBN 978-0-8146-6452-0   ISBN 978-0-8146-6476-6 (e-book)
Exodus, Part Two: ISBN 978-0-8146-6453-7   ISBN 978-0-8146-6477-3 (e-book)

TABLE OF CONTENTS

Wrap-up lectures are available for each lesson at no charge. The link to these free lectures is LittleRockScripture.org/Lectures/ExodusPartTwo.

Welcome

The Bible is at the heart of what it means to be a Christian. It is the Spirit-inspired word of God for us. It reveals to us the God who created, redeemed, and guides us still. It speaks to us personally and as a church. It forms the basis of our public liturgical life and our private prayer lives. It urges us to live worthily and justly, to love tenderly and wholeheartedly, and to be a part of building God's kingdom here on earth.

Though it was written a long time ago, in the context of a very different culture, the Bible is no relic of the past. Catholic biblical scholarship is among the best in the world, and in our time and place, we have unprecedented access to it. By making use of solid scholarship, we can discover much about the ancient culture and religious practices that shaped those who wrote the various books of the Bible. With these insights, and by praying with the words of Scripture, we allow the words and images to shape us as disciples. By sharing our journey of faithful listening to God's word with others, we have the opportunity to be stretched in our understanding and to form communities of love and learning. Ultimately, studying and praying with God's word deepens our relationship with Christ.

Exodus, Part Two
Exodus 16–40

The resource you hold in your hands is divided into four lessons. Each lesson involves personal prayer and study using this book *and* the experience of group prayer, discussion, and wrap-up lecture.

If you are using this resource in the context of a small group, we suggest that you meet four times, discussing one lesson per meeting. Allow about 90 minutes for the small group gathering. Small groups function best with eight to twelve people to ensure good group dynamics and to allow all to participate as they wish.

WHAT MATERIALS WILL YOU USE?

The materials in this book include:

- The text of Exodus, chapters 16–40, using the New American Bible, Revised Edition as the translation.

- Commentary by Stephen J. Binz, which has also been published separately as *The God of Freedom and Life: A Commentary on the Book of Exodus* (Liturgical Press).

- Occasional inserts 🔥 highlighting elements of the chapters of Exodus being studied. Some of these appear also in the *Little Rock Catholic Study Bible* while others are supplied by staff writers.

- Questions for study, reflection, and discussion at the end of each lesson.

- Opening and closing prayers for each lesson, as well as other prayer forms available in the closing pages of the book.

In addition, there are wrap-up lectures available for each lesson. Your group may choose to purchase a DVD containing these lectures or make use of the audio or video lectures online at no charge. The link to these free lectures is: LittleRockScripture.org/Lectures/ExodusPartTwo. Of course, if your group has access to qualified speakers, you may choose to have live presentations.

Each person will need a current translation of the Bible. We recommend the *Little Rock Catholic Study Bible*, which makes use of the New American Bible, Revised Edition. Other translations, such as the New Jerusalem Bible or the New Revised Standard Version: Catholic Edition, would also work well.

HOW WILL YOU USE THESE MATERIALS?

Prepare in advance

Using Lesson One as an example:

- Begin with a simple prayer like the one found on page 11.

- Read the assigned material in the printed book for Lesson One (pages 12–19) so that you are prepared for the weekly small group session. You may do this assignment by reading a portion over a period of several days (effective and manageable) or by preparing all at once (more challenging).

- Answer the questions, Exploring Lesson One, found at the end of the assigned reading, pages 20–22.

- Use the Closing Prayer on page 23 when you complete your study. This prayer may be used again when you meet with the group.

Meet with your small group

- After introductions and greetings, allow time for prayer (about 5 minutes) as you begin the group session. You may use the prayer found on page 11 (also used by individuals in their preparation) or use a prayer of your choosing.

- Spend about 45–50 minutes discussing the responses to the questions that were prepared in advance. You may also develop your discussion further by responding to questions and interests that arise during the discussion and faith-sharing itself.

- Close the discussion and faith-sharing with prayer, about 5–10 minutes. You may use the Closing Prayer at the end of each lesson or one of your choosing at the end of the book. It is important to allow people to pray for personal and community needs and to give thanks for how God is moving in your lives.

- Listen to or view the wrap-up lecture associated with each lesson (15–20 minutes). You may watch the lecture online, use a DVD, or provide a live lecture by a qualified local speaker. This lecture provides a common focus for the group and reinforces insights from each lesson. You may view the lecture together at the end of the session or, if your group runs out of time, you may invite group members to watch the lecture on their own time after the discussion.

Above all, be aware that the Holy Spirit is moving within and among you.

Exodus

Part Two

LESSON ONE

Introduction and Exodus 16–18

Begin your personal study and group discussion with a simple and sincere prayer such as:

Prayer

> *God of the exodus, give us a share in the freedom and life you offer. As we read and study your word, free our minds to understand you and enliven our hearts to love you.*

Read the Introduction on page 12 and the Bible text of Exodus 16–18 found in the outside columns of pages 13–19, highlighting what stands out to you.

Read the accompanying commentary to add to your understanding.

Respond to the questions on pages 20–22, Exploring Lesson One.

The Closing Prayer on page 23 is for your personal use and may be used at the end of group discussion.

INTRODUCTION

Welcome to our study of Exodus, Part Two (Exodus 16–40). The book of Exodus is a foundational book of Scripture. Its message about YHWH (the LORD) as a God who hears the cry of the oppressed, liberates them, and enters freely into a covenant relationship with them is essential to the Jewish and Christian understanding of who God is and what it means to be God's people.

The book of Exodus as it currently appears in our Bibles is the product of generations of Israelites telling and retelling these stories of faith, followed by a centuries-long process of writing, compiling, and editing. Modern scholars have identified at least four strands of tradition woven together into the book of Exodus: the Yahwist, the Elohist, the Deuteronomist, and the Priestly traditions (see Exodus, Part One for more information about each one). These traditions can be detected throughout the Pentateuch (the first five books of the Bible) and give witness to the richness of Israel's journey with God and the development of Israelite faith over time.

In our study of Exodus, Part One (Exodus 1–15), we encountered the Israelites enduring "cruel slavery" (1:13) at the hands of Pharaoh of Egypt. "Mindful of his covenant with Abraham, Isaac and Jacob" (2:24), God heard the cries of his people and called upon Moses to go to Pharaoh and demand the release of all Israelites from Egypt.

An epic story of struggle and rescue ensued as Pharaoh repeatedly refused to free the Israelites, finally relenting after a series of plagues that climaxed in the tenth and final plague: the death of firstborns all over Egypt (12:29-32). Having marked their doors with the blood of a lamb, the Israelites were spared the effects of this deadly plague as the LORD "passed over" their homes, and they were set free by Pharaoh to "[g]o and serve the LORD" (12:31). Although Pharaoh and his army changed their minds and pursued the Israelites, they were drowned by the waters of the Red Sea after the Israelites safely crossed on dry land.

In this rich saga of Exodus 1–15, we learned that YHWH is never far from his people. God desires freedom and life, not oppression and cruelty. No earthly power is strong enough to defeat this God of freedom and life or to thwart God's plans of liberation for Israel.

In Part Two of our study, we will continue to journey with the Israelites through the desert toward the land the LORD has promised them. There will be grumbling and complaining (16:2), fickleness and idolatry (32:8), violence and loss (32:28). But there will also be powerful signs of the LORD's presence (19:18), a prophet who speaks to God face to face (33:11), an eternal covenant forged between God and human beings (24:7), and the fantastic construction of a portable sanctuary (39:32). Through fidelity to covenant law and worship, Israel will bind herself ever closer to YHWH, the God of freedom and life.

16:1-3 The Wilderness of Sin

Just as thirst had led to the Israelites' grumbling at Marah (15:22-27), their hunger prompted their complaining in the Desert of Sin. Presumably after traveling through the desert for a month, they had consumed the provisions with which they had left Egypt. They had not yet learned where to turn for their source of life, so they looked back with longing to the table of Pharaoh. Facing all the uncertainties that freedom creates, the Israelite community regrets their redemption and desires to return to the security of slavery.

16:4-15 The Quail and the Manna

Human griping is contrasted with divine generosity. The "grumbling" of the Israelites is mentioned six times in verses 7-12. Remarkably, God does not respond with severity, but the complaints of Israel become the springboard for God's display of grace. Yhwh promises flesh in the evening and bread in the morning so that the people of Israel might know Yhwh as the one who generously sustains their life.

In the seventh plague, God rained down hail upon Egypt, destroying the sources of food; now God will "rain down bread from heaven" to provide for the hunger of God's people. In the eighth plague, the arrival of the

CHAPTER 16

The Wilderness of Sin

¹Having set out from Elim, the whole Israelite community came into the wilderness of Sin, which is between Elim and Sinai, on the fifteenth day of the second month after their departure from the land of Egypt. ²Here in the wilderness the whole Israelite community grumbled against Moses and Aaron. ³The Israelites said to them, "If only we had died at the Lord's hand in the land of Egypt, as we sat by our kettles of meat and ate our fill of bread! But you have led us into this wilderness to make this whole assembly die of famine!"

The Quail and the Manna

⁴Then the Lord said to Moses: I am going to rain down bread from heaven for you. Each day the people are to go out and gather their daily portion; thus will I test them, to see whether they follow my instructions or not. ⁵On the sixth day, however, when they prepare what they bring in, let it be twice as much as they gather on the other days. ⁶So Moses and Aaron told all the Israelites, "At evening you will know that it was the Lord who brought you out of the land of Egypt; ⁷and in the morning you will see the glory of the Lord, when he hears your grumbling against him. But who are we that you should grumble against us?" ⁸And Moses said, "When the Lord gives you meat to eat in the evening and in the morning your fill of bread, and hears the grumbling you utter against him, who then are we? Your grumbling is not against us, but against the Lord." ⁹Then Moses said to Aaron, "Tell the whole Israelite community: Approach the Lord, for he has heard your grumbling." ¹⁰But while Aaron was speaking to the whole Israelite community, they turned in the direction of the wilderness, and there the glory of the Lord appeared in the cloud! ¹¹The Lord said to Moses: ¹²I have heard the grumbling of the Israelites. Tell them: In the evening twilight you will eat meat, and in the

continue

morning you will have your fill of bread, and then you will know that I, the LORD, am your God.

¹³In the evening, quail came up and covered the camp. In the morning there was a layer of dew all about the camp, ¹⁴and when the layer of dew evaporated, fine flakes were on the surface of the wilderness, fine flakes like hoarfrost on the ground. ¹⁵On seeing it, the Israelites asked one another, "What is this?" for they did not know what it was. But Moses told them, "It is the bread which the LORD has given you to eat."

Regulations Regarding the Manna

¹⁶"Now, this is what the LORD has commanded. Gather as much of it as each needs to eat, an omer for each person for as many of you as there are, each of you providing for those in your own tent." ¹⁷The Israelites did so. Some gathered a large and some a small amount. ¹⁸But when they measured it out by the omer, the one who had gathered a large amount did not have too much, and the one who had gathered a small amount did not have too little. They gathered as much as each needed to eat. ¹⁹Moses said to them, "Let no one leave

continue

locusts that came and covered the land is described in the same way as the arrival of the quail that covered the camp and provided food. When Israel abides in freedom with God and relies on divine providence, the necessities of life abound.

The ancient authors do not imply that the gifts of manna and quail were inexplicable occurrences. The thin flaky substance that the writer compares with hoarfrost may very well be the secretions of the tamerisk plant or the excretions of the insects that feed on its fruit. Still gathered today by the nomads of the desert, the sugary substance accumulates during the cool of the night and disintegrates in the heat of the day. The quail may be migratory birds that are often exhausted enough to be caught by hand when they land.

The Priestly tradition does not emphasize the mere fact of this desert food; the text, rather, accentuates what the people learned about YHWH from their experience. In the desert they came to realize that God bestows numerous blessings in the context of their daily lives. God's presence is not to be sought after in the extraordinary, in strange and inexplicable events. Rather, divine generosity is discovered in all that contributes to Israel's life. YHWH is

In the **Bread of Life Discourse** (John 6:22-59), Jesus compares himself to the manna eaten by the Israelites. Consider this exchange between Jesus and those who questioned him:

³⁰So [the crowd] said to [Jesus], "What sign can you do, that we may see and believe in you? What can you do? ³¹Our ancestors ate manna in the desert, as it is written:
'He gave them bread from heaven to eat.'"

³²So Jesus said to them, "Amen, amen, I say to you, it was not Moses who gave the bread from heaven; my Father gives you the true bread from heaven. ³³For the bread of God is that which comes down from heaven and gives life to the world."

³⁴So they said to him, "Sir, give us this bread always." ³⁵Jesus said to them, "I am the bread of life; whoever comes to me will never hunger, and whoever believes in me will never thirst. . . . ⁴⁹"Your ancestors ate the manna in the desert, but they died; ⁵⁰this is the bread that comes down from heaven so that one may eat it and not die. ⁵¹I am the living bread that came down from heaven; whoever eats this bread will live forever; and the bread that I will give is my flesh for the life of the world" (John 6:30-35, 49-51).

intimately involved in the daily needs of this new community of God's people.

16:16-36 Regulations Regarding the Manna

Yhwh gives Israel the necessities of life. Manna sustains the people with the gift of nourishment; the Sabbath favors Israel with necessary rest and renewal. Yet with God's gifts also comes responsibility. The gifts of freedom bring the necessity of discipline. Thus, God tests the Israelites so that God's generosity becomes the occasion for Israel to develop a responsible lifestyle.

The people were to gather only their daily portion of manna. They were to gather it in such a way that everyone had enough to eat and no one had too little. They were not to store the manna or accumulate it for the future; they were to rely on God for the needs of each day.

Setting aside one day each week as special is also a way of living responsibly as a free people. The Sabbath, as a day of solemn rest, expresses the fact that Israel's days of bondage are over. Disengaging from work as a day of hallowed leisure is an opportunity to break from the daily routine of life and an expression of harmony with God's creative design for life. The double portion of manna to be collected on the sixth day insures that daily needs are satisfied while obeying the regulations of the Sabbath.

God's command to preserve a daily provision of manna for posterity will serve as a remembrance of God's care in forming the community of Israel. The enduring memory of the daily "bread from heaven" is to replace their distorted memory of the bread of Egypt (v. 3). The instruction anticipates the command to build the ark of the covenant and the sanctuary in the wilderness to be described later in the text. The jar of manna will be placed in front of the tablets of God's commandments. A sign of God's compassionate care (the manna) and a sign of God's law for Israel (the tablets of the commandments) are to be associated together in Israel's worship.

any of it over until morning." [20]But they did not listen to Moses, and some kept a part of it over until morning, and it became wormy and stank. Therefore Moses was angry with them.

[21]Morning after morning they gathered it, as much as each needed to eat; but when the sun grew hot, it melted away. [22]On the sixth day they gathered twice as much food, two omers for each person. When all the leaders of the community came and reported this to Moses, [23]he told them, "That is what the LORD has prescribed. Tomorrow is a day of rest, a holy sabbath of the LORD. Whatever you want to bake, bake; whatever you want to boil, boil; but whatever is left put away and keep until the morning." [24]When they put it away until the morning, as Moses commanded, it did not stink nor were there worms in it. [25]Moses then said, "Eat it today, for today is the sabbath of the LORD. Today you will not find any in the field. [26]Six days you will gather it, but on the seventh day, the sabbath, it will not be there." [27]Still, on the seventh day some of the people went out to gather it, but they did not find any. [28]Then the LORD said to Moses: How long will you refuse to keep my commandments and my instructions? [29]Take note! The LORD has given you the sabbath. That is why on the sixth day he gives you food for two days. Each of you stay where you are and let no one go out on the seventh day. [30]After that the people rested on the seventh day.

[31]The house of Israel named this food manna. It was like coriander seed, white, and it tasted like wafers made with honey.

[32]Moses said, "This is what the LORD has commanded. Keep a full omer of it for your future generations, so that they may see the food I gave you to eat in the wilderness when I brought you out of the land of Egypt." [33]Moses then told Aaron, "Take a jar and put a full omer of manna in it. Then place it before the LORD to keep it for your future generations." [34]As the LORD had commanded Moses, Aaron placed it in front of the covenant to keep it.

continue

35The Israelites ate the manna for forty years, until they came to settled land; they ate the manna until they came to the borders of Canaan. 36(An omer is one tenth of an ephah.)

CHAPTER 17

Water from the Rock

1From the wilderness of Sin the whole Israelite community journeyed by stages, as the LORD directed, and encamped at Rephidim.

But there was no water for the people to drink, 2and so they quarreled with Moses and said, "Give us water to drink." Moses replied to them, "Why do you quarrel with me? Why do you put the LORD to a test?" 3Here, then, in their thirst for water, the people grumbled against Moses, saying, "Why then did you bring us up out of Egypt? To have us die of thirst with our children and our livestock?" 4So Moses cried out to the LORD, "What shall I do with this people? A little more and they will stone me!" 5The LORD answered Moses: Go on ahead of the people, and take along with you some of the elders of Israel, holding in your hand, as you go, the staff with which you struck the Nile. 6I will be standing there in front of you on the rock in Horeb. Strike the rock, and the water will flow from it for the people to drink. Moses did this, in the sight of the elders of Israel. 7The place was named Massah and Meribah, because the Israelites quarreled there and tested the LORD, saying, "Is the LORD in our midst or not?"

Battle with Amalek

8Then Amalek came and waged war against Israel in Rephidim. 9So Moses said to Joshua, "Choose some men for us, and tomorrow go out and engage Amalek in battle. I will be standing on top of the hill with the staff of God in my hand." 10Joshua did as Moses told him: he engaged Amalek in battle while Moses, Aaron, and Hur climbed to the top of the hill. 11As long as Moses kept his hands raised up, Israel had the better of the fight, but when he let his hands rest,

continue

17:1-7 Water from the Rock

The crisis that developed at this stage of the journey is described as the people's "quarrel" with Moses and their "test" of YHWH. Fearing a rebellion and even his own death by stoning, Moses intercedes with God and once again God graciously sustains the life of Israel. The tradition associated the incident with the place names by which the event was remembered. Massah means a "place of testing" and Meribah means a "place of quarreling."

The people of Israel demonstrate a lack of trust in YHWH's providential care for them. Testing YHWH means demanding that God demonstrate concretely and prove to them the divine presence. Verse 7 focuses the issue on the question, "Is the LORD in our midst or not?" The question is incredible in view of God's deliverance of Israel from slavery, God's rescue at the sea, and God's direction and sustenance in the wilderness. As the psalmist sang of YHWH, "they tried [tested] me though they had seen my works" (Ps 95:9).

In this desert land where life is so precarious and death is always threatening, God works through Moses and his staff to provide water for the people. Moses' striking the rock to bring water for the people to drink is the life-giving counterpart to Moses' striking the Nile to make the water unfit to drink in the land of bondage. The tradition of Israel saw much more significance in these events than satisfying physical needs. YHWH is the Rock upon whom the pilgrim people rely; the flowing water is the life that God constantly provides for them.

17:8-16 Battle with Amalek

The Amalekites were a wide-ranging desert tribe who would be enemies of Israel for many generations. The hostilities that began in the wilderness would continue into the land of promise and not end until the time of Israel's monarchy. They attacked at a time of great vulnerability for Israel, seeking to exterminate this newborn people. Like a new Pharaoh in the wilderness, Amalek threatened the freedom and life God had won for Israel. Such threatening powers will continually be a part of Israel's history and Israel's victories over them credited to God.

Again, Moses is the instrument of God's victory for Israel. His raised staff and his devoted presence on top of the hill is a visible expression of Yhwh's presence in the battle. Moses' hands held aloft invited Israel to trust in Yhwh and became an efficacious sign of the power of God at work in saving the life of Israel.

Joshua is first introduced here as Israel's commander in combat. His name means "Yhwh delivers." This battle is the first of many in which Joshua will lead the people of Israel in conquering the land promised to them. His very name indicates that Israel's successes are determined not by her own strength but through human cooperation with God's will.

The altar that commemorated this event was named "Yahweh-nissi" or "The Lord is my standard." The raised standard or banner for Israel was the firm and steady presence of Moses with his hands outstretched. To remember the raised hands of Moses standing as a banner on the hilltop was to recall that the hand of God would be active in Israel's deliverance through the centuries.

18:1-12 Meeting with Jethro

In contrast to the hostility of the Amalekites, the Midianites became friends and allies with Israel through the family ties with Moses. The name of Moses' elder son recalls the condition of God's people at his son's birth, "a resident alien in a foreign land." The name of his second son expresses the new experience of God's people, "the God of my father is my help." The text implies that Moses had sent his family back to Midian when conditions grew worse in Egypt. Now that Yhwh has rescued Israel, they are able to be reunited. This moment of reunion becomes an opportunity to look back and rejoice at what God had already accomplished before beginning the momentous events at Mount Sinai.

The focus is on Jethro, Moses' father-in-law, whom Moses greets with deep respect and

Amalek had the better of the fight. ¹²Moses' hands, however, grew tired; so they took a rock and put it under him and he sat on it. Meanwhile Aaron and Hur supported his hands, one on one side and one on the other, so that his hands remained steady until sunset. ¹³And Joshua defeated Amalek and his people with the sword.

¹⁴Then the Lord said to Moses: Write this down in a book as something to be remembered, and recite it to Joshua: I will completely blot out the memory of Amalek from under the heavens. ¹⁵Moses built an altar there, which he named Yahweh-nissi; ¹⁶for he said, "Take up the banner of the Lord! The Lord has a war against Amalek through the ages."

CHAPTER 18

Meeting with Jethro

¹Now Moses' father-in-law Jethro, the priest of Midian, heard of all that God had done for Moses and for his people Israel: how the Lord had brought Israel out of Egypt. ²So his father-in-law Jethro took along Zipporah, Moses' wife—now this was after Moses had sent her back—³and her two sons. One of these was named Gershom; for he said, "I am a resident alien in a foreign land." ⁴The other was named Eliezer; for he said, "The God of my father is my help; he has rescued me from Pharaoh's sword." ⁵Together with Moses' wife and sons, then, his father-in-law Jethro came to him in the wilderness where he was encamped at the mountain of God, ⁶and he sent word to Moses, "I, your father-in-law Jethro, am coming to you, along with your wife and her two sons."

⁷Moses went out to meet his father-in-law, bowed down, and then kissed him. Having greeted each other, they went into the tent. ⁸Moses then told his father-in-law of all that the Lord had done to Pharaoh and the Egyptians for the sake of Israel, and of all the hardships that had beset them on their journey, and how the Lord had rescued them. ⁹Jethro rejoiced over all the goodness that the Lord had shown Israel in

continue

rescuing them from the power of the Egyptians. [10]"Blessed be the LORD," he said, "who has rescued you from the power of the Egyptians and of Pharaoh. [11]Now I know that the LORD is greater than all the gods; for he rescued the people from the power of the Egyptians when they treated them arrogantly." [12]Then Jethro, the father-in-law of Moses, brought a burnt offering and sacrifices for God, and Aaron came with all the elders of Israel to share with Moses' father-in-law in the meal before God.

Appointment of Minor Judges

[13]The next day Moses sat in judgment for the people, while they stood around him from morning until evening. [14]When Moses' father-in-law saw all that he was doing for the people, he asked, "What is this business that you are conducting for the people? Why do you sit alone while all the people have to stand about you from morning till evening?" [15]Moses answered his father-in-law, "The people come to me to consult God. [16]Whenever they have a disagreement, they come to me to have me settle the matter between them and make known to them God's statutes and instructions."

[17]"What you are doing is not wise," Moses' father-in-law replied. [18]"You will surely wear yourself out, both you and these people with you. The task is too heavy for you; you cannot do it alone.

continue

affection. The experience of Jethro's coming to faith in YHWH becomes the pattern for entry into the faith community of Israel. First, Moses declares all the mighty acts that God has done for Israel. Having heard the good news proclaimed to him, Jethro rejoices. He then makes his own confession of faith in YHWH, offers sacrifices, and shares with the people of Israel in a sacred meal.

18:13-27 Appointment of Minor Judges

This text gives some of the oldest indications concerning the formation of Israel's legal traditions. Freedom brought with it the necessity of living responsibly, and a system for promoting justice within the community inevitably developed. The narrative associates Israel's legal system with the covenant to be established at Sinai and makes clear that YHWH is the source and authority of both the law of Israel and its interpretation in the course of Israel's daily life.

In Israel, there was no distinction between divine law and civil law. All of the decisions and regulations that bind Israel as God's people were understood to be related to the covenant that God established with Israel. The covenant was made applicable to the countless problems that inevitably arise in daily existence.

The counsel that Jethro gave Moses is first of all an affirmation of Moses' role as intermediary between God and the people. Moses is to bring the concerns and problems of Israel before God in order to discern the will of God in their daily lives. He is also to be the teacher of Israel, bringing to them an understanding of God's law and clarifying God's expectations. Secondly, Jethro's counsel is practical advice about delegation of authority. Moses is counseled to appoint trustworthy officials over various divisions of people to make judgments for them. The more general and less complex disputes would be handled by these judges, while the more difficult problems would be brought to Moses. This arrangement may reflect a later period in Israel's history where matters for which there was some precedence were handled locally while unique problems that would require a new application of covenant principles would be brought to court in Jerusalem. The narrative makes clear that the developing system of justice always looked back to Moses and the covenant as its original source.

[19]Now, listen to me, and I will give you some advice, and may God be with you. Act as the people's representative before God, and bring their disputes to God. [20]Enlighten them in regard to the statutes and instructions, showing them how they are to conduct themselves and what they are to do. [21]But you should also look among all the people for able and God-fearing men, trustworthy men who hate dishonest gain, and set them over the people as commanders of thousands, of hundreds, of fifties, and of tens. [22]Let these render decisions for the people in all routine cases. Every important case they should refer to you, but every lesser case they can settle themselves. Lighten your burden by letting them bear it with you! [23]If you do this, and God so commands you, you will be able to stand the strain, and all these people, too, will go home content."

[24]Moses listened to his father-in-law and did all that he had said. [25]He picked out able men from all Israel and put them in charge of the people as commanders of thousands, of hundreds, of fifties, and of tens. [26]They rendered decisions for the people in all routine cases. The more difficult cases they referred to Moses, but all the lesser cases they settled themselves. [27]Then Moses said farewell to his father-in-law, who went off to his own country.

EXPLORING LESSON ONE

1. The Israelites hold Moses and Aaron responsible for their meager provisions (16:2-3). Why do you suppose we sometimes slip so easily into blame rather than trust or cooperation?

_____

_____

_____

_____

_____

2. What "desert experiences" have at first seemed impossible but later proved to be blessings for you (16:3)?

_____

_____

_____

_____

_____

3. a) What does it say about God's desires and expectations for Israel that the people were to collect only enough manna for one day at a time (16:19)? (See Matt 6:25-34.)

_____

_____

_____

b) How does the "daily portion" of manna given to Israel (16:4) help you to understand the "daily bread" we pray for in the Lord's Prayer (Matt 6:9-13)?

_____

_____

_____

4. In what ways is Jesus the true manna? (See John 6:30-35, 49-51.)

_____

_____

_____

_____

_____

5. What is the purpose of rest on the Sabbath (16:23)? (See 20:8-11; 31:14-17.) In what ways does this Sabbath command challenge you personally?

_____

_____

_____

_____

_____

6. What, if anything, causes you to ask the question, "Is the LORD in our midst or not?" (17:7)? (See Ps 95:8-9.)

When I come face to face with injustice or poverty; When I think about the holocaust or other terrible evil existing in the world.

_____

_____

_____

7. How does Moses' role during the battle with Amalek (17:8-13) foreshadow the role of Jesus on our behalf? (See Rom 8:34; Heb 4:14—5:3; 1 John 2:1-2.)

Moses was an intermediary between God, the father and the Hebrew people; Jesus is our intermediary between God and ourselves. Both interceded for the people to the Father. Both acted as high priest in time of need Jesus like Moses is an intercessor for us to God, the father.

8. What pattern of actions in 18:9-12 is similar to that of the Mass? (For similar patterns, see 2 Sam 6:17-19 and Luke 24:25-30.)

David, like Moses fed the Israelites. Jesus, like Moses, feeds His people. Eucharist is like Manna from heaven

_____

_____

_____

9. The growth of a community of believers presents challenges related to authority and organization. Moses faced this problem (18:13-16) as did the apostles in the early church (see Acts 6:1-6). How are the two solutions similar?

Authority was delegated to other good men because it was too much for Moses or for the apostles. Good men were chosen from among the people. Deacons

10. a) Why did Moses listen to Jethro, a Midianite priest and non-Israelite, on a matter of religious authority (18:13-24)?

He trusted Jethro with his family; he was an elder; Jethro brought a burnt offering although he was not an Israelite; he was a priest. His argument made sense.

b) What might this say about problem-solving in the church today?

Rome seems to be delegating more authority to local bishops; even at the parish level more of the laity are involved in parish decisions, such as parish councils, teaching authority, charity work. One priest cannot do it all.

CLOSING PRAYER

Prayer

*The LORD said to Moses: I have heard the
grumbling of the Israelites. Tell them:
In the evening twilight you will eat meat,
and in the morning you will have your fill
of bread, and then you will know that I,
the LORD, am your God.* (Exod 16:11-12)

Lord God, you cared for your people as they traveled
through the desert. When they were thirsty, you gave
them fresh water. When they were hungry, you fed them
with manna and quails. Nourish us and quench our
thirst as we study your word. Assure us that you are
always with us, and that you provide us with everything we need. We pray for those in special need of the
good things you provide, especially . . .

LESSON TWO

Exodus 19–24

Begin your personal study and group discussion with a simple and sincere prayer such as:

Prayer

God of the exodus, give us a share in the freedom and life you offer. As we read and study your word, free our minds to understand you and enliven our hearts to love you.

Read the Bible text of Exodus 19–24 found in the outside columns of pages 26–41, highlighting what stands out to you.

Read the accompanying commentary to add to your understanding.

Respond to the questions on pages 42–44, Exploring Lesson Two.

The Closing Prayer on page 45 is for your personal use and may be used at the end of group discussion.

VI. Covenant and Legislation at Mount Sinai

CHAPTER 19

Arrival at Sinai

¹In the third month after the Israelites' departure from the land of Egypt, on the first day, they came to the wilderness of Sinai. ²After they made the journey from Rephidim and entered the wilderness of Sinai, they then pitched camp in the wilderness.

While Israel was encamped there in front of the mountain, ³Moses went up to the mountain of God. Then the LORD called to him from the mountain, saying: This is what you will say to the house of Jacob; tell the Israelites: ⁴You have seen how I treated the Egyptians and how I bore you up on eagles' wings and brought you to myself. ⁵Now, if you obey me completely and keep my covenant, you will be my treasured possession among all peoples, though all the earth is mine. ⁶You will be to me a kingdom of priests, a holy nation. That is what you must tell the Israelites. ⁷So Moses went and summoned the elders of the people. When he set before them all that the LORD had ordered him to tell them, ⁸all the people answered together, "Everything the LORD has said, we will do." Then Moses brought back to the LORD the response of the people.

⁹The LORD said to Moses: I am coming to you now in a dense cloud, so that when the people hear me speaking with you, they will also remain faithful to you.

When Moses, then, had reported the response of the people to the LORD, ¹⁰the LORD said to Moses: Go to the people and have them sanctify themselves today and tomorrow. Have them wash their garments ¹¹and be ready for the third day; for on the third day the LORD will come down on Mount Sinai in the sight of all the people. ¹²Set limits for the people all around, saying: Take care not to go up the mountain, or even to touch its edge. All who touch the mountain must be put

continue

19:1-15 Arrival at Sinai

As the people of Israel reach Mount Sinai, the narrative returns to its source. Anticipated since Moses' experience of YHWH at the burning bush, the movement of Exodus has been to bring Israel to this place of encounter with God. Here God will come to meet Israel and reveal the divine nature more fully, just as God had come to meet Moses to reveal the divine name. Here the people will stay throughout the remainder of the book of Exodus until the journey continues in Numbers 10:11.

The religious tradition of Israel attached tremendous importance to the covenant-making at Sinai. The covenant that God forms with Israel here will formally bind them in a relationship that will determine the entire subsequent history of Israel. Unlike their bondage in Egypt under Pharaoh, the covenant with YHWH will be life-giving and characterized by mutual freedom. Renewed continually throughout history, the covenant became the characteristic feature of Israel's religion.

Verses 3-8 serve as a prologue for all the events that will happen at Sinai and they are a summary of Israel's understanding of covenant. The elevated style and structure of these verses seem to characterize the passage as part of a periodic ceremony of covenant reenactment and renewal. First, there is a proclamation of God's mighty deeds (v. 4); second, the conditions of the covenant are set forth (vv. 5-6); and finally, the people give their free response of commitment (vv. 7-8). This is the pattern that dominates all of Israel's subsequent ceremonies of covenant renewal (Josh 24).

The invitation to covenant is based on God's saving deeds in the past. God is here described as an eagle bearing its young to the mountain. Further developed in Deuteronomy 32:10-11, the image is one of nurture and protection, in which the parent eagle tenderly cares for its young and hovers over them. It is also an image of testing and maturation, in which the eagle helps the young to fly for themselves by catching them as they fall from the nest and bearing them on its outstretched wings. The image is one of gentle encouragement, preferring to elicit a free response from people rather than imposing submission by force.

The conditions for this relationship with God call for Israel to hearken to God's voice and keep God's covenant. It is a personal invitation to experience life more fully, based on the faithfulness that God has already shown in the past. With an affirmative response, the people of Israel would be described by three separate but interrelated images. As God's "treasured possession" among all other people, Israel would be like the crown jewel of a king's treasure. As a "kingdom of priests" Israel would have special access to Yhwh and would serve as mediators between God and other kingdoms. As a "holy nation" Israel would be set apart from others for the worship and service of God.

Israel's response, "Everything the Lord has said, we will do," indicates the people's enthusiastic acceptance of this relationship with God. It is a pledge to a God to whom they are already closely related. The remaining events at Sinai will unfold the implications of their commitment and reveal more fully the nature of this life-giving God of the covenant.

Moses is instructed to prepare the people for the theophany to come. The text does not specify all that is involved in this sanctification of the people, only that they are to wash their garments and refrain from sexual intercourse.

to death. [13]No hand shall touch them, but they must be stoned to death or killed with arrows. Whether human being or beast, they must not be allowed to live. Only when the ram's horn sounds may they go up on the mountain. [14]Then Moses came down from the mountain to the people and had them sanctify themselves, and they washed their garments. [15]He said to the people, "Be ready for the third day. Do not approach a woman."

The Great Theophany

[16]On the morning of the third day there were peals of thunder and lightning, and a heavy cloud over the mountain, and a very loud blast of the

continue

This consecration involves a separation from what is normal and good in daily existence to prepare for an extraordinary encounter with the divine. The mountain too is to be sanctified ground to which no one may approach except Moses. Setting up of ritual boundaries and ritual purification reflects practices later in Israel's history in which people were sealed off from the sacred precincts of the temple and were prepared for cultic ceremonies.

The "third day," the time of God's manifestation on the mountain, indicates a brief period of time marked by rising anticipation. When the ram's horn sounds, the call both to war and to worship throughout Israel's history, the people may approach the boundary set up by Moses. Yhwh would come in the dense cloud and speak to Moses, thereby affirming him as the mediator of God's word. The many trips of Moses up and down the mountain reinforce his role as mediator of the covenant.

19:16-25 The Great Theophany

The coming of Yhwh begins at daybreak on the third day. In ancient cultures the mountain was the place of divine encounter, a bridge between earth and the heavens. The thunder and lightning, the heavy cloud, the fire and shofar, so that all the people in the camp trembled. ¹⁷But Moses led the people out of the camp to meet God, and they stationed themselves at the foot of the mountain. ¹⁸Now Mount Sinai was completely enveloped in smoke, because the LORD had come down upon it in fire. The smoke rose from it as though from a kiln, and the whole mountain trembled violently. ¹⁹The blast of the shofar grew louder and louder, while Moses was speaking and God was answering him with thunder.

²⁰When the LORD came down upon Mount Sinai, to the top of the mountain, the LORD summoned Moses to the top of the mountain, and Moses went up. ²¹Then the LORD told Moses: Go down and warn the people not to break through to the LORD in order to see him; otherwise many of them will be struck down. ²²For their part, the priests, who approach the LORD must sanctify themselves; else the LORD will break out in anger against them. ²³But Moses said to the LORD, "The people cannot go up to Mount Sinai, for you yourself warned us, saying: Set limits around the mountain to make it sacred." ²⁴So the LORD said to him: Go down and come up along with Aaron. But do not let the priests and the people break through to come up to the LORD; else he will break out against them." ²⁵So Moses went down to the people and spoke to them.

CHAPTER 20

The Ten Commandments

¹Then God spoke all these words:
²I am the LORD your God, who brought you out of the land of Egypt, out of the house of slavery. ³You shall not have other gods beside me. ⁴You shall not make for yourself an idol or a likeness of anything in the heavens above or on the earth below or in the waters beneath the earth; ⁵you shall not bow down before them or serve them. For I, the LORD, your God, am a jealous God, inflicting punishment for their ancestors' wickedness on the children of those who hate me,

continue

smoke, and the trembling mountain are all biblical expressions for divine power and the manifestation of God's presence. As Moses leads the procession of the people to the mountain, the increasing blast of the ram's horn gives rising intensity to the awesome scene.

 A **theophany** is a manifestation of God, a sign of God's presence. Common images for theophanies are fire, light, and cloud.

It is impossible to distinguish what happened at the historical event and the later re-enactment of the event in the covenant renewal. The cultic ceremony as it developed in Israel would have involved a procession to the holy place accompanied by the sounding of trumpets and clouds of incense rising from the sanctuary. For the Hebrew there was only one covenant event in which every ritual renewal shared; thus the passage reflects elements of Israel's worship developed through the centuries.

20:1-17 The Ten Commandments

Although the Decalogue is often taken out of its biblical context for liturgical and catechetical reasons, it is important to see that God's commandments are an integral part of the Sinai narrative. They flow out of the action of God's self-revelation and God's liberating activity among the people of Israel. God's instructions for the life of the community are centered in the self-identification of the living and freeing God. God's commandments, which could have been understood as another form of bondage for Israel, are understood as the gracious instruction of the God who leads them through obedience to greater freedom and fuller life.

Since the Sinai narrative is all about the unique interpersonal relationship that God established with Israel, the law is understood to be a gift of God's generosity and an opportunity for Israel to personally respond to what

God has done on her behalf. For every generation, responding to God's commandments, just as worshiping God in liturgy, would be a way of sharing in the redeeming actions of the Exodus and living in the covenant.

The experience of Egypt had shown how the subversion of God's will had created bondage, oppression, and death. The law of Israel is given so that the experience of Egypt will not be repeated among them. Thus, the Ten Commandments flow from Yhwh "who brought you out of the land of Egypt, out of the house of slavery." When the law is obeyed in love, it promotes and enhances the quality of life that God desires for the people of Israel and it guarantees that they will continue to live in freedom.

The list of Ten Commandments (literally, "ten words," 34:28; Deut 4:13; 10:4) originally consisted of ten brief imperatives. Their collection in this simple, easy-to-remember form kept them alive in the community through the ages. In time, these brief words were expanded as the general principles were applied in new ways to respond to particular needs.

These commandments were not intended to be comprehensive. They were the foundation and starting point for the ongoing task of ethical reflection among the newborn people. Yet the privileged status of these ten among all the laws of Israel is emphasized by the narrative. These are the words spoken by Yhwh in the hearing of all the people as they gathered around the sacred mountain. They are laws dealing with the most important principles and boundaries that would define life within covenant and community.

Although the tradition that the commandments are ten in number is strong, various communities have arranged the numbering differently through the centuries. The sequence of commandments varies within Jewish tradition and the Ten Commandments are never isolated from the larger body of biblical law in the rabbinical writings. The Catholic tradition generally treats verses 3-6 as a single commandment and Deuteronomy 5:21 as two precepts. The Reformed tradition treats verses

down to the third and fourth generation; [6]but showing love down to the thousandth generation of those who love me and keep my commandments.

[7]You shall not invoke the name of the LORD, your God, in vain. For the LORD will not leave unpunished anyone who invokes his name in vain.

[8]Remember the sabbath day—keep it holy. [9]Six days you may labor and do all your work, [10]but the seventh day is a sabbath of the LORD your God. You shall not do any work, either you, your son or your daughter, your male or female slave, your work animal, or the resident alien within your gates. [11]For in six days the LORD made the heavens and the earth, the sea and all that is in them; but on the seventh day he rested. That is why the LORD has blessed the sabbath day and made it holy.

[12]Honor your father and your mother, that you may have a long life in the land the LORD your God is giving you.

[13]You shall not kill.

[14]You shall not commit adultery.

[15]You shall not steal.

[16]You shall not bear false witness against your neighbor.

[17]You shall not covet your neighbor's house. You shall not covet your neighbor's wife, his male or female slave, his ox or donkey, or anything that belongs to your neighbor.

continue

4-6 as the second commandment and considers verse 17 (Deut 5:21) as the tenth commandment.

The first commandment enjoins Israel to an exclusive relationship with Yhwh. The command does not indicate that Israel's earliest belief was absolute monotheism—the understanding that there is only one God for the whole world. Israel, however, was to live in absolute and singular loyalty to Yhwh, thus rejecting a relationship with all other gods.

The prohibition against creating idols was originally intended to forbid the creation of any images of Yhwh for Israel's worship. The purpose was to protect Israel's understanding of Yhwh as the God who exists in total freedom. God's self-revelation was through the divine word acting in Israel's history. They were to worship Yhwh without compromising the transcendent yet personal divine presence by an image that could be contained and confined. The imageless cult of Israel set her off from all the other surrounding cultures. God's presence and power could not be controlled by the use of images or any other technique of worship. Israel always used verbal images of God because they have the capacity to express God's relatedness in ways that static images do not.

The prohibition was later expanded to include images of foreign gods. The challenge of Canaanite religion constantly tempted Israel to pervert religion into an activity for obtaining blessings from God. Yhwh is described as "jealous," a metaphor from the sphere of marriage. Unfaithfulness to the commitment with God is contagious for the next generations and thus evokes the righteous anger of God for several generations. In contrast, commitment to the covenant evokes unlimited goodness generation after generation.

The prohibition against using the name of God for empty and useless purposes was to protect the sacredness of the divine name. God's name, either the revealed name "Yhwh" or any of the divine titles by which Israel called upon God, was to be invoked, honored, and praised. The divine name expressed the very nature of God that Israel was privileged to have continually revealed to her. Abuse of the divine name was seen to be so serious that the commandment was expanded later in history to contain a solemn warning for disobedience.

The "sabbath" was a day of "stopping," a day of cessation from the normal daily routine. For Israel this day was to be made "holy," set aside for something special, as a day belonging to Yhwh. This is the most expanded of all the commandments, with clauses added through the centuries to justify and apply this central tenet of Israel's life. The Priestly tradition added the justification in verse 11 connecting the Sabbath with God's creation. Yet the pattern of the seven days in the creation account of Genesis 1 is patterned on the fact that Israel already kept this seventh day as a day of rest. The Priestly writer thus ties the Sabbath observance with God's rhythmical plan for all of life. Israelites, slaves, animals, and foreigners are all to cease from labor on the Sabbath.

An earlier tradition associated the Sabbath with Israel's experience of liberation. While in slavery there was no interruption of the unending round of forced labor. Moses' request for time to worship God in the desert was met with scorn by Pharaoh. The Sabbath became a remembrance for Israel of her former slavery and God's deliverance (Deut 5:15). Thus, the Sabbath was understood by Israel as a divine gift related directly to the God who created life and the God who gave Israel freedom.

To "honor" one's parents meant to demonstrate a respect and reverence that is usually reserved for God. Honor for God is the foundation of the covenant; honor for fathers and mothers is the foundation of all other human relationships. The commandment refers to the reverence and care adults must show toward their elderly parents and to the respectful obedience children must offer their mother and father. God is the giver of all life, so parents together are the channel of that life to their children. The promise of long life and prosperity associated with the commandment assures that one's own life is enhanced by honoring the bearers of that life.

Since human life is such a sacred gift, to take a life is forbidden. The negative imperative forbids acts of death-dealing violence that arise out of vengeance, malice, anger, or desire for personal gain. Though usually intended to describe intentional killing, or murder, the verb is also used to describe unintentional killing. Since God is the giver and lord of life, Israel developed many laws designed to insure that human life was protected within the covenant community.

The command against adultery is intended to protect the sanctity of the marriage bond and refers to either the man or the woman as the subject. The offense is a crime not only against the human relationship but it also affects the covenant with God in a serious way. Faithfulness to the marital relationship reflected faithfulness to the covenant with YHWH. Like the worship of other gods, adultery was a turning away from commitment to YHWH. The severe penalty of death attached to adultery in Israel's legal tradition indicates the seriousness of the rupture it creates.

The prohibition against stealing is the third in a series of commands that consist of two Hebrew words: a negative particle and a four-letter verb form without a definite object. Many think that these simple negative imperatives were the original form of many of the commandments. The prohibition indicates that Israel understood theft of a person's property as a violation against the person. Those in covenant with YHWH are not to steal because disruption of relationships within community also disrupts one's relationship with God.

The command against false witness was the foundation of Israel's legal process. The communal institution of justice depended on truthfulness. Yet the testimony one gives before the elders in a legal proceeding is not something separate from the witness one gives in all the other circumstances of communal life. The term "neighbor" refers to a fellow member of the covenant community. The prohibition was understood to refer to any lie that harms the reputation of a neighbor, whether it be slanderous or deceptive talk or damaging rumor about another. Not only individuals but the well-being of community is damaged by a lack of trustworthiness among its members.

The final commandment refers to a subjective attitude, whereas the previous prohibitions were directed against an objective action. The verb translated "covet" means to desire obsessively or lust after for oneself. "Neighbor's house" includes everything connected with the fullness of life of one who is in covenant community: one's entire family and one's entire property. The command was expanded to specify what covetousness meant in the context

 Ten Commandments: Two Versions

1. I am the LORD your God; you shall have no strange gods.	Exod 20:2-6	Deut 5:6-11
2. You shall not take the name of God in vain.	Exod 20:7	Deut 5:11
3. Remember to keep holy the Sabbath day. *Different reasons*: God rested on the seventh day (Exod 20:11); you were once slaves (Deut 5:15).	Exod 20:8-11	Deut 5:12-15
4. Honor your father and your mother.	Exod 20:12	Deut 5:16
5. You shall not kill.	Exod 20:13	Deut 5:17
6. You shall not commit adultery.	Exod 20:14	Deut 5:18
7. You shall not steal.	Exod 20:15	Deut 5:19
8. You shall not bear false/dishonest witness against your neighbor.	Exod 20:16	Deut 5:20
9.–10. You shall not covet. *Different order*: Your neighbor's house, his wife, or anything else (Exod 20:17); Your neighbor's wife, slave, animals, or anything else (Deut 5:21).	Exod 20:17	Deut 5:21

Moses Accepted as Mediator

[18]Now as all the people witnessed the thunder and lightning, the blast of the shofar and the mountain smoking, they became afraid and trembled. So they took up a position farther away [19]and said to Moses, "You speak to us, and we will listen; but do not let God speak to us, or we shall die." [20]Moses answered the people, "Do not be afraid, for God has come only to test you and put the fear of him upon you so you do not sin." [21]So the people remained at a distance, while Moses approached the dark cloud where God was.

The Covenant Code

[22]The LORD said to Moses: This is what you will say to the Israelites: You have seen for yourselves that I have spoken to you from heaven. [23]You shall not make alongside of me gods of silver, nor shall you make for yourselves gods of gold. [24]An altar of earth make for me, and sacrifice upon it your burnt offerings and communion sacrifices, your sheep and your oxen. In every place where I cause my name to be invoked I will come to you and bless you. [25]But if you make an altar of stone for me, do not build it of cut stone, for by putting a chisel to it you profane it. [26]You shall not ascend to my altar by steps, lest your nakedness be exposed.

continue

of covenant community. Deuteronomy 5:21 detached "wife" into a separate commandment for unknown reasons.

The subjective attitude of covetousness often leads to objective misuse of what is not one's own. It is an attitude of discontent that leads to violation of the other commandments. It thus serves as a summary warning because of its comprehensiveness and its reference to the interior disposition that can lead to social disorder.

The Ten Commandments not only place boundaries on the community of Israel but also encourage the development of the covenant. The law expresses Israel's commitment to be faithful to the Exodus experience. Though the precepts are formulated negatively, they implicitly commend their positive side. For example, not abusing God's name invites praise of God, not killing implies efforts to respect life, not committing adultery encourages faithful relationships in marriage, and not bearing false witness suggests honoring the good name of others. Israel recognized that the integrity of the covenant demanded mutual respect for persons—for their life, their relationships, their reputation, and their belongings.

20:18-21 Moses Accepted as Mediator

Overwhelmed by the astonishing and dreadful experience of the divine presence, the people withdrew in trembling fear. They confirm Moses' role as the intermediary between God and the people. Previously, Moses had been set apart and made mediator of the covenant by God's choice. Now, the people affirm his role by requesting that he take their place before the divine presence and then report to them the words of YHWH.

His intercessory role continues throughout the Exodus tradition as Moses becomes the suffering mediator of his people. He not only speaks for God to Israel but he also represents Israel before God. As mediator he will receive the additional laws that follow (20:23ff.), seal the covenant with YHWH (24:1ff.), plead for Israel at the golden calf episode (32:1ff.), and finally, die outside the Promised Land because of the sin of the people (Deut 1:37).

The divine self-manifestation amidst awesome spectacle is not designed to impose a trembling fear but to evoke a reverential fear within the people. Moses urges the people, "Do not be afraid, for God has come only to test you and put the fear of him upon you so you do not sin." With this kind of respect for their relationship with YHWH, the people would be able to hold the divine law expressed in these commands as the focal priority of their lives.

20:22-26 The Covenant Code

This section begins a long collection of laws, continuing through 23:33, called the Book of the Covenant (24:7). These verses serve to link the complex of laws to the experience at Sinai. Though Moses communicates the law to Israel, the covenant regulations clearly have their origin in YHWH. Obedience to the law, then, is not a matter of outward adherence to an impersonal theory of justice but a response to a personal God who has entered into a relationship with Israel and calls them to order all of their communal life under this covenant.

The first law defines the essence of Israel's faithfulness: exclusive worship of YHWH alone. This loyalty to YHWH is the foundation of all the other regulations, which are multiple expressions of that singular loyalty. The instructions concerning the altar continue this concern for proper worship. It stipulates that altars of sacrifice are to be made from the earth. When they are made from stone, they are not to be cut with tools. No explicit reasons are given for these specifications, though they are probably designed to distinguish Israel's worship from that of surrounding cultures. Altars are to be constructed at those places chosen by divine initiative; therefore, multiple sanctuaries are allowed throughout the land, but only at places of legitimate worship.

At these sanctuaries, God promises to come and bless the worshipers. Israel's cult is the setting in which God's presence can be experienced with certainty and focused intensity. Israel can be loyal to God only because God assures divine loyalty to them. This context of worship and blessings provides the setting for Israel's life of obedience to God. The God who gives commandments to be obeyed is also the God who makes promises.

21:1-11 Laws Regarding Slaves

The designation given for the laws that follow is "rules" or "ordinances." These are best understood as guiding decisions or precedent cases that draw out the implications of the Ten Commandments in the practical order. These judgments apply the generally stated principles to the specific issues that need attention within a particular time and context.

CHAPTER 21

Laws Regarding Slaves

[1]These are the ordinances you shall lay before them. [2]When you purchase a Hebrew slave, he is to serve you for six years, but in the seventh year he shall leave as a free person without any payment. [3]If he comes into service alone, he shall leave alone; if he comes with a wife, his wife shall leave with him. [4]But if his master gives him a wife and she bears him sons or daughters, the woman and her children belong to her master and the man shall leave alone. [5]If, however, the slave declares, 'I love my master and my wife and children; I will not leave as a free person,' [6]his master shall bring him to God and there, at the door or doorpost, he shall pierce his ear with an awl, thus keeping him as his slave forever.

[7]When a man sells his daughter as a slave, she shall not go free as male slaves do. [8]But if she displeases her master, who had designated her for himself, he shall let her be redeemed. He has no right to sell her to a foreign people, since he has broken faith with her. [9]If he designates her for his son, he shall treat her according to the ordinance for daughters. [10]If he takes another wife, he shall not withhold her food, her clothing, or her conjugal rights. [11]If he does not do these three things for her, she may leave without cost, without any payment.

continue

In responding justly to specific situations, God's compassionate care for Israel becomes the paradigm for Israel's treatment of others. As God cared for the oppressed, showing them how to live in freedom, so Israel is to show compassion for others. God will continue to hear the cries of the oppressed as Israel continues to enter into the suffering of those in need.

Slavery was an accepted institution within the society of Israel. The ordinances concern the treatment of slaves, giving guidance for the

Personal Injury

[12]Whoever strikes someone a mortal blow must be put to death. [13]However, regarding the one who did not hunt another down, but God caused death to happen by his hand, I will set apart for you a place to which that one may flee. [14]But when someone kills a neighbor after maliciously scheming to do so, you must take him even from my altar and put him to death. [15]Whoever strikes father or mother shall be put to death.

[16]A kidnapper, whether he sells the person or the person is found in his possession, shall be put to death.

[17]Whoever curses father or mother shall be put to death.

[18]When men quarrel and one strikes the other with a stone or with his fist, not mortally, but enough to put him in bed, [19]the one who struck the blow shall be acquitted, provided the other can get up and walk around with the help of his staff. Still, he must compensate him for his recovery time and make provision for his complete healing.

[20]When someone strikes his male or female slave with a rod so that the slave dies under his hand, the act shall certainly be avenged. [21]If, however, the slave survives for a day or two, he is not to be punished, since the slave is his own property.

[22]When men have a fight and hurt a pregnant woman, so that she suffers a miscarriage, but no further injury, the guilty one shall be fined as much as the woman's husband demands of him, and he shall pay in the presence of the judges. [23]But if injury ensues, you shall give life for life, [24]eye for eye, tooth for tooth, hand for hand, foot for foot, [25]burn for burn, wound for wound, stripe for stripe.

[26]When someone strikes his male or female slave in the eye and destroys the use of the eye, he shall let the slave go free in compensation for the eye. [27]If he knocks out a tooth of his male or female slave, he shall let the slave go free in compensation for the tooth.

continue

care of both male (vv. 2-6) and female (vv. 7-11) slaves. Hope for freedom was to live in the heart of those held in servitude. The major stipulation of the law stated that a slave was to be released in the seventh year. This provision is followed by several "if" clauses that introduce particular refinements of the law. One may become a permanent slave under his own volition because of devotion to his family and his owner.

The law is different for female slaves since they often became the wives or concubines of their owners. They were not to be released in the seventh year (though this seems to be changed later in Deut 15:12). The owner may take her for himself, give her to his son as a wife, or let her be redeemed by her family. The conditions for each case specify certain rights of female slaves and protection from inhumane treatment. If any of these rights are violated, she is to be given her freedom.

21:12-32 Personal Injury

This series of rules deals with those inflicting harm on others. Situations calling for the death penalty are listed first (vv. 12-17), followed by those calling for lesser penalties. The penalty of death is imposed for these offenses: murder, stealing another person for sale into slavery, and striking or cursing one's parent.

Verse 13 makes a distinction between murder and accidental death. If a fatal blow to another is not preplanned, the perpetrator may go to a place of sanctuary from the death penalty. Though the place of sanctuary is not specified, the reference to God's altar in verse 14 seems to indicate that the place of safety was any altar of Yhwh.

Actions inflicting less serious damage on the community are more numerous. The general principle guiding such personal injuries is the law of retaliation (vv. 23-25). This legal principle guards against unbridled revenge by insisting on proportionate compensation for injuries. It also provides greater equality before the law for those of lower social status. The wealthy were not allowed to merely pay a fine for injury done.

Slaves, however, do not qualify for equal compensation for harm done to them. Yet the concern for slaves in the law is remarkably humanitarian for the ancient world. If a master injures a slave, whether with the loss of an eye or a tooth, the slave is to be freed. When a slave is mistreated, the slave becomes an oppressed person and therefore ought to be liberated.

21:33–22:5 Property Damage

These laws deal with damage to property resulting from negligence, theft, and fire. The general principle for these crimes against property is proper restitution. The payment in money or kind to be given to the one wronged is often greater than the damage caused. In the case of theft of an ox or sheep, the thief is to pay fivefold for an ox and fourfold for a sheep. A thief who cannot make restitution is to be sold into slavery to pay for his theft.

22:6-14 Trusts and Loans

These rules deal with various cases involving loss or theft of property put in the care of another. Those to whom property is entrusted must be aware of their own liability. When something of value is missing when an owner comes to claim it, a thief must be sought. If one is found, the case is simply resolved by requiring a double compensation from the thief. If a thief is not found, the one who accepted the trust must be brought into the presence of God so that his innocence or culpability may be established.

The judicial process is closely linked to the religious aspects of Israel's life. Verses 7, 8, and 10 indicate that God enters into the process and attends personally to matters of justice. The decision is rendered in the sanctuary, either by a divine oracle or by a judge who has authority to speak divine judgments. The process also involves an oath before God with the understanding that YHWH as witness to the oath was its guarantor.

22:15–23:9 Social Laws

Sexual promiscuity is condemned in Israel because it fails to protect the exploited person

28When an ox gores a man or a woman to death, the ox must be stoned; its meat may not be eaten. The owner of the ox, however, shall be free of blame. 29But if an ox was previously in the habit of goring people and its owner, though warned, would not watch it; should it then kill a man or a woman, not only must the ox be stoned, but its owner also must be put to death. 30If, however, a fine is imposed on him, he must pay in ransom for his life whatever amount is imposed on him. 31This ordinance applies if it is a boy or a girl that the ox gores. 32But if it is a male or a female slave that it gores, he must pay the owner of the slave thirty shekels of silver, and the ox must be stoned.

Property Damage

33When someone uncovers or digs a cistern and does not cover it over again, should an ox or a donkey fall into it, 34the owner of the cistern must make good by restoring the value of the animal to its owner, but the dead animal he may keep.
35When one man's ox hurts another's ox and it dies, they shall sell the live ox and divide this money as well as the dead animal equally between them. 36But if it was known that the ox was previously in the habit of goring and its owner would not watch it, he must make full restitution, an ox for an ox; but the dead animal he may keep.
37When someone steals an ox or a sheep and slaughters or sells it, he shall restore five oxen for the one ox, and four sheep for the one sheep.

CHAPTER 22

1[If a thief is caught in the act of housebreaking and beaten to death, there is no bloodguilt involved. 2But if after sunrise he is thus beaten, there is bloodguilt.] He must make full restitution. If he has nothing, he shall be sold to pay for his theft. 3If what he stole is found alive in his possession, be it an ox, a donkey or a sheep, he shall make twofold restitution.

continue

⁴When someone causes a field or a vineyard to be grazed over, by sending his cattle to graze in another's field, he must make restitution with the best produce of his own field or vineyard. ⁵If a fire breaks out, catches on to thorn bushes, and consumes shocked grain, standing grain, or the field itself, the one who started the fire must make full restitution.

Trusts and Loans

⁶When someone gives money or articles to another for safekeeping and they are stolen from the latter's house, the thief, if caught, must make twofold restitution. ⁷If the thief is not caught, the owner of the house shall be brought to God, to swear that he himself did not lay hands on his neighbor's property. ⁸In every case of dishonest appropriation, whether it be about an ox, or a donkey, or a sheep, or a garment, or anything else that has disappeared, where another claims that the thing is his, the claim of both parties shall be brought before God; the one whom God convicts must make twofold restitution to the other.

⁹When someone gives an ass, or an ox, or a sheep, or any other animal to another for safekeeping, if it dies, or is maimed or snatched away, without anyone witnessing the fact, ¹⁰there shall be an oath before the LORD between the two of them that the guardian did not lay hands on his neighbor's property; the owner must accept the oath, and no restitution is to be made. ¹¹But if the guardian has actually stolen from it, then he must make restitution to the owner. ¹²If it has been killed by a wild beast, let him bring it as evidence; he need not make restitution for the mangled animal.

¹³When someone borrows an animal from a neighbor, if it is maimed or dies while the owner is not present, that one must make restitution. ¹⁴But if the owner is present, that one need not make restitution. If it was hired, this was covered by the price of its hire.

continue

from the social consequences. The seduction of an unengaged maiden impaired her chances for a respectable marriage by taking away her virginity. Thus, the man is required to take full responsibility for his action by paying the customary marriage price and by marrying the girl. If the father of the girl opposes the marriage, the seducer must still pay a sum equivalent to the marriage price.

The laws beginning with verse 17 return to the apodictic form: "You [whoever] shall (not) . . ." The contemporary practice of separating religious, social, and personal ethics do not hold for Israel's legislation. Verses 17-19 deal with three offenses calling for the death penalty. The sorceress was identified with pagan practice because she sought to interpret and control the future, thus escaping or altering the will and work of YHWH. Copulation with an animal is condemned because of its association with fertility worship among the surrounding cultures. Sacrificing to another god is a violation against the first commandment, and like the other two offenses, is a direct affront to YHWH.

Verses 20-26 reflect an intense concern for the disadvantaged and weakest members of society. Resident aliens, those living in a community other than their own, are classified with widows and orphans as needing special protection. Without security and family support and without a husband and father, they were vulnerable to abuse and exploitation. Mistreatment of the defenseless members of society calls forth the wrath of YHWH. The reverse side of God's compassion is the severe divine judgment for those who are victimizers.

If the poor are forced to borrow money, the one who advances money is not to charge interest. If collateral is held by the creditor, it is to be returned before it causes hardship. The cloak taken by the creditor is to be returned before sundown because it serves as the bedding for the impoverished one. The poor are to be treated, thus, as fellow members of the covenant family of God.

These commands are accompanied by exhortation. The motivation for obedience is found by repeated reference to the experience of Exodus (22:20; 23:9). When the people of Israel mistreat the disadvantaged, they violate their own history and disavow those saving acts of liberation that made them who they are. Those who received the gift of freedom and life must continue to extend those gifts to others.

The principle of avoiding injustice and listening to the cries of the oppressed is an invitation to extend these laws to ever new situations. Changing historical and social circumstances challenge Israel to constantly revise these particular rules and apply the principles in new ways. Ongoing discernment of God's will continued to adapt these guiding decisions for the society of Israel as new occasions taught new responsibilities.

Verses 27-30 may be classified as holiness laws, which set Israel apart as sacred to YHWH. The people must never show any disrespect for YHWH. And they must not curse a leader of the covenant community, for such an act would demonstrate contempt for the divine authority given him. Holding back that to which God is entitled, whether from the fields, the vineyards, the womb, the herd or flock, is also an act of disrespect for YHWH. The joyous and generous offering of the firstfruits, the firstborn sons, and the firstborn animals is a worthy act of thanksgiving to God.

The first verses of chapter 23 give admonitions concerning Israel's judicial system. Those involved in a trial must not give false testimony or spread rumors that would prejudice the case; they must not follow the majority view to the detriment of justice; and they must not accept a bribe. They are obliged to acquit the innocent and condemn the guilty, being careful not to give an unfair advantage to the poor, and giving the needy and the alien their full rights (Lev 19:15).

Verses 4-5 challenge the people of Israel to realize that justice, such as the return of lost goods and offering assistance to one in need, is due even to one's personal enemies. The covenant offers a new perspective toward all people in need, and obedience to the covenant means refusing to take advantage of another's misfortune because he happens to be an enemy.

Social Laws

[15]When a man seduces a virgin who is not betrothed, and lies with her, he shall make her his wife by paying the bride price. [16]If her father refuses to give her to him, he must still pay him the bride price for virgins.

[17]You shall not let a woman who practices sorcery live.

[18]Anyone who lies with an animal shall be put to death.

[19]Whoever sacrifices to any god, except to the LORD alone, shall be put under the ban.

[20]You shall not oppress or afflict a resident alien, for you were once aliens residing in the land of Egypt. [21]You shall not wrong any widow or orphan. [22]If ever you wrong them and they cry out to me, I will surely listen to their cry. [23]My wrath will flare up, and I will kill you with the sword; then your own wives will be widows, and your children orphans.

[24]If you lend money to my people, the poor among you, you must not be like a money lender; you must not demand interest from them. [25]If you take your neighbor's cloak as a pledge, you shall return it to him before sunset; [26]for this is his only covering; it is the cloak for his body. What will he sleep in? If he cries out to me, I will listen; for I am compassionate.

[27]You shall not despise God, nor curse a leader of your people.

[28]You shall not delay the offering of your harvest and your press. You shall give me the firstborn of your sons. [29]You must do the same with your oxen and your sheep; for seven days the firstling may stay with its mother, but on the eighth day you must give it to me.

[30]You shall be a people sacred to me. Flesh torn to pieces in the field you shall not eat; you must throw it to the dogs.

CHAPTER 23

[1]You shall not repeat a false report. Do not join your hand with the wicked to be a witness

continue

supporting violence. ²You shall not follow the crowd in doing wrong. When testifying in a lawsuit, you shall not follow the crowd in perverting justice. ³You shall not favor the poor in a lawsuit.

⁴When you come upon your enemy's ox or donkey going astray, you must see to it that it is returned. ⁵When you notice the donkey of one who hates you lying down under its burden, you should not desert him; you must help him with it.

⁶You shall not pervert justice for the needy among you in a lawsuit. ⁷You shall keep away from anything dishonest. The innocent and the just you shall not put to death, for I will not acquit the guilty. ⁸Never take a bribe, for a bribe blinds the clear-sighted and distorts the words of the just. ⁹You shall not oppress a resident alien; you well know how it feels to be an alien, since you were once aliens yourselves in the land of Egypt.

Religious Laws

¹⁰For six years you may sow your land and gather in its produce. ¹¹But the seventh year you shall let the land lie untilled and fallow, that the poor of your people may eat of it and their leftovers the wild animals may eat. So also shall you do in regard to your vineyard and your olive grove. ¹²For six days you may do your work, but on the seventh day you must rest, that your ox and your donkey may have rest, and that the son of your maidservant and resident alien may be refreshed. ¹³Give heed to all that I have told you.

You shall not mention the name of any other god; it shall not be heard from your lips.

¹⁴Three times a year you shall celebrate a pilgrim feast to me. ¹⁵You shall keep the feast of Unleavened Bread. As I have commanded you, you must eat unleavened bread for seven days at the appointed time in the month of Abib, for it was then that you came out of Egypt. No one shall appear before me empty-handed. ¹⁶You shall also keep the feast of the grain harvest with the first fruits of the crop that you sow in the field; and

continue

23:10-19 Religious Laws

The pattern of the Sabbath year is the same as that of the Sabbath day. In the year of rest, after six years of sowing and harvesting, the land is to be left alone. This applies to the cultivation of grain fields as well as the pruning and harvesting of the vineyards and olive orchards. Though the original motivation for this year is uncertain, it receives various explanations throughout the Hebrew Scriptures. In Exodus, the motivation of social concern comes to the fore. Whatever the land produces without cultivation, the poor of the land are to have, and whatever they leave, the animals are to have.

Likewise, the seventh day is motivated by concern for the refreshment of all, including the poor, the alien, and the animals. Worship of God and ritual concerns are not separated from wider human concerns and issues of justice.

Verse 13 forms a summary statement urging obedience to all the rules that have been stated. It also reinforces Israel's central command prohibiting worship of any deity except Yhwh alone. The presence of God in every sphere of life is emphasized by all the ordinances that have preceded and by the three pilgrim feasts that mark key moments in the yearly agricultural cycle of Israel's existence.

The feast of Unleavened Bread, in the spring, marked the time of the first harvest, the barley harvest planted in winter. The feast is here associated with the yearly commemoration of the Exodus. Pilgrimage to the shrine included an offering of some of the first grain in thanksgiving to Yhwh. The feast of the grain harvest marked the harvest of the wheat crop seven weeks later. Later tradition called this the feast of Weeks (or Sevens) or Pentecost, because it occurred on the fiftieth day. Jewish tradition associated the feast with the giving of the Law. The feast of the fruit harvest was the largest festival of thanksgiving, occurring in autumn as the final ingathering. It was later called the feast of Booths (or Tabernacles or Tents), commemorating Israel's time of nomadic wandering in the wilderness.

Other miscellaneous instructions relate to Israel's ritual. Leaven was seen as an impurity and was unfit for use in sacrifice. The fat of the sacrificial animal, like the blood, was to be offered to God and burned entirely. Boiling a kid in its mother's milk was a Canaanite practice that was seen as abhorrent by Israel.

23:20-33 Reward of Fidelity

God assures Israel of the blessings of the divine presence on their journey to the Promised Land. "Angel," as in 3:2 and 14:19, is any form under which God's guiding and protecting presence is experienced by Israel. God's blessings are manifested in those things that provide abundant life for Israel: deliverance from enemies (vv. 22-24), nourishment and health (v. 25), fertility and long life (v. 26), and secure possession of the land (v. 27).

The land to be entered and settled by Israel is anticipated in this section: its conquest, its blessings, its magnitude, and its purity from the worship of other gods. Though YHWH promised that Israel would inherit the land, it would be a gradual possession. The extent of the land is an idealized projection that was never historically realized, even during the time of David and Solomon.

The Book of the Covenant ends as it began, with the command for exclusive devotion to YHWH. All that lies between are the many and varied ways of expressing that devotion in the life of Israel. The first commandment is the binding theme that makes such a diverse collection of ordinances a singular code.

24:1-11 Ratification of the Covenant

This chapter concludes the narrative of Sinai that began in chapter 19. The teaching conveyed through God's revelation to Moses is now shared with the people. Israel responds faithfully and a solemn covenant relationship is ratified with appropriate ritual. Israel's leaders are then given further authorization for their ongoing role by receiving an intimate experience of YHWH's presence as they eat the covenant meal.

finally, the feast of Ingathering at the end of the year, when you collect your produce from the fields. [17]Three times a year shall all your men appear before the LORD God.

[18]You shall not offer the blood of my sacrifice with anything leavened; nor shall the fat of my feast be kept overnight till the next day. [19]The choicest first fruits of your soil you shall bring to the house of the LORD, your God.

You shall not boil a young goat in its mother's milk.

Reward of Fidelity

[20]See, I am sending an angel before you, to guard you on the way and bring you to the place I have prepared. [21]Be attentive to him and obey him. Do not rebel against him, for he will not forgive your sin. My authority is within him. [22]If you obey him and carry out all I tell you, I will be an enemy to your enemies and a foe to your foes.

[23]My angel will go before you and bring you to the Amorites, Hittites, Perizzites, Canaanites, Hivites and Jebusites; and I will wipe them out. [24]Therefore, you shall not bow down to their gods and serve them, nor shall you act as they do; rather, you must demolish them and smash their sacred stones. [25]You shall serve the LORD, your God; then he will bless your food and drink, and I will remove sickness from your midst; [26]no woman in your land will be barren or miscarry; and I will give you a full span of life.

[27]I will have the terror of me precede you, so that I will throw into panic every nation you reach. I will make all your enemies turn from you in flight, [28]and ahead of you I will send hornets to drive the Hivites, Canaanites and Hittites out of your way. [29]But I will not drive them all out before you in one year, lest the land become desolate and the wild animals multiply against you. [30]Little by little I will drive them out before you, until you have grown numerous enough to take possession of the land. [31]I will set your boundaries

from the Red Sea to the sea of the Philistines, and from the wilderness to the Euphrates; all who dwell in this land I will hand over to you and you shall drive them out before you. ³²You shall not make a covenant with them or their gods. ³³They must not live in your land. For if you serve their gods, this will become a snare to you.

CHAPTER 24

Ratification of the Covenant

¹Moses himself was told: Come up to the LORD, you and Aaron, with Nadab, Abihu, and seventy of the elders of Israel. You shall bow down at a distance. ²Moses alone is to come close to the LORD; the others shall not come close, and the people shall not come up with them.

³When Moses came to the people and related all the words and ordinances of the LORD, they all answered with one voice, "We will do everything that the LORD has told us." ⁴Moses then wrote down all the words of the LORD and, rising early in the morning, he built at the foot of the mountain an altar and twelve sacred stones for the twelve tribes of Israel. ⁵Then, having sent young men of the Israelites to offer burnt offerings and sacrifice young bulls as communion offerings to the LORD, ⁶Moses took half of the blood and put it in large bowls; the other half he splashed on the altar. ⁷Taking the book of the covenant, he read it aloud to the people, who answered, "All that the LORD has said, we will hear and do." ⁸Then he took the blood and splashed it on the people, saying, "This is the blood of the covenant which the LORD has made with you according to all these words."

⁹Moses then went up with Aaron, Nadab, Abihu, and seventy elders of Israel, ¹⁰and they beheld the God of Israel. Under his feet there appeared to be sapphire tilework, as clear as the sky itself. ¹¹Yet he did not lay a hand on these chosen Israelites. They saw God, and they ate and drank.

continue

A threefold gradation is made: Moses alone, the chosen mediator between God and Israel, is to come close to God on the mountain; Aaron, two of his sons, and seventy elders of Israel are to accompany Moses up the mountain but remain at a distance; and the people are not to climb up the mountain at all. The purpose of the leaders' approach is to worship YHWH. Though verses 1-2 fit better with verses 9-11, the final editor has sandwiched verses 3-8. The covenant ritual with all the people was placed within the context of God's manifested presence to those leaders chosen to enact and interpret God's revelation.

Moses reported all the "words" and "ordinances" of YHWH, the Ten Commandments along with the guiding principles of the law. After the people committed themselves to God by their freely acclaimed assent, Moses wrote down all the words to define the legal terms of the covenant agreement. He then set up the altar and twelve pillars to represent the relationship being established between each of the tribes and YHWH.

The sacrifices offered were of two kinds: the "burnt offerings" or holocausts, the offerings that were completely burned on the altar, and "communion offerings," the fat of which was burned and the rest shared among the participants as a sacrificial meal. The blood of the sacrifice both symbolized and contained life (Lev 17:14). Pouring the blood on the altar was the sign that YHWH was the Lord of life. When Moses then proclaimed from the Book of the Covenant, he was proclaiming the words of the God of life. The people's commitment joined them with this God who was the source of their new life. The splashing of sacrificial blood on the people established a community of life between YHWH and Israel. The "blood of the covenant" (v. 8) is the seal and pledge of this relationship. The people of Israel are now called to the task of living the quality of life that the covenant entails.

The intimate contact of Israel's leaders with their God (v. 9ff.) prepares them for their service of teaching and judging. The vision of God on the mountain is awe-inspiring and full of mystery beyond the power of words to express. The rich sapphire pavement at God's feet suggests the blueness of the heavens. The sight of the tile work may indicate that they were prostrate before God and did not lift their faces, since no one could do so and live (33:20). The divine effulgence indicated a real and personal presence of God with Moses and the leaders of the people as they celebrated the communion meal. The sacrificial banquet on the mountain implied a real sharing of life between YHWH and Israel.

24:12-18 Moses on the Mountain

This scene provides the context for the next large section of material—the instructions for the divine tabernacle (chaps. 25–31). God's command for Moses to ascend the mountain and receive the stone tablets will be concluded in 31:18 as God gives the two tablets that Moses then brings down the mountain in 32:15. The mention of Joshua as Moses' attendant anticipates his subsequent role in chapter 32. Aaron and Hur are asked to wait below along with the elders to deal with any problems that might arise. Their charge sets the stage for the disaster to follow in chapter 32.

The Priestly tradition provides the material that begins in verse 15 and continues throughout the instructions for the tabernacle. The "glory of the LORD," the visible manifestation of God, is priestly language. This glory is shown in the descending cloud and the consuming fire seen by the people on the mountaintop. This appearance of God in cloud and fire will characterize God's presence in the tabernacle at the end of Exodus (40:38). What happened at Sinai will be continued at the tabernacle.

Moses on the Mountain

[12]The LORD said to Moses: Come up to me on the mountain and, while you are there, I will give you the stone tablets on which I have written the commandments intended for their instruction. [13]So Moses set out with Joshua, his assistant, and went up to the mountain of God. [14]He told the elders, "Wait here for us until we return to you. Aaron and Hur are with you. Anyone with a complaint should approach them." [15]Moses went up the mountain. Then the cloud covered the mountain. [16]The glory of the LORD settled upon Mount Sinai. The cloud covered it for six days, and on the seventh day he called to Moses from the midst of the cloud. [17]To the Israelites the glory of the LORD was seen as a consuming fire on the top of the mountain. [18]But Moses entered into the midst of the cloud and went up on the mountain. He was on the mountain for forty days and forty nights.

EXPLORING LESSON TWO

1. Based on what you have studied so far, how would you sum up the experience of the Israelites as they wandered in the desert? Try to condense it to just a few phrases.

rebelious, complaining, looking backward to what they had in Egypt; They were led out of slavery, but showed that they preferred what they had known to what future God had in store for them.

2. What are the reasons for the cleansing and prohibitions in 19:9-15, 21-25?

Cleansing [body + garments] was to sanctify themselves; Do not go up the mountain, or be stoned or killed with arrows; do not touch a woman. To prove their obedience to God through obedience to Moses' instruction. But God did not mention touching a woman?

3. Write the Ten Commandments (20:1-17) in your own words in one of the following ways:

   • Write the commandments in a positive way rather than as prohibitions.

   • Write how you would concretely live out several of the commandments (e.g., "Honor your father and your mother" may mean "calling my dad once a week" or "telling my mom I love her").

   • Write the commandments in a way that would make sense to children or teens.

1. Worship only me. Covenant with God is exclusive
2. Say my name in prayer, not abusing it?
3. Honor me on the Sabbath. It is a day of rest
4. Ensure a long + fruitful life by honoring parents + in childhood, obey parents
5. Honor + protect life which is a gift from God.
6. Ensure the sanctity of family life by faithfulness to vows
7. Respect the belongings of others as theirs.
8. Be truthful in all your dealings with others.
9. Dwell on the blessings you already have.
10. Be grateful for the committed relations you have, Respect the marriage vows of others.

4. How do the Ten Commandments (20:1-17) correspond to Jesus' commands in Mark 12:28-34? (See Lev 19:17-18; Deut 6:4-5.)

first 3 commandment are about our relationship to God; all the others are about our relation to eachother. The first & Second of the Greatest commandments Leviticus 19 has to do with our relation and others Deuteronomy 6 is about relationship of God + man. We are to love him with all our heart & with all our soul + strength

5. Why is it significant that the giving of the Ten Commandments begins with the words "I am the LORD your God, who brought you out of the land of Egypt, out of the house of slavery" (20:2)?

This is a reminder of what God has already done for the Israelites: bringing them out of slavery into freedom lest they forget (which they did after.

6. What kind of fear is induced by God's revelation (20:20)? (See Ps 19:9; Prov 1:7.)

They feared they would die.

7. Slavery was an accepted institution in the ancient world. How do the provisions in 21:1-11 begin to challenge this institution?

A Hebrew slave is held for six years, then released.

8. The provisions in 21:12-32 are meant to discourage the Israelites from harming one another by laying out a clear punishment for each offense. How does Jesus' message about retaliation provide an extreme contrast to these provisions (Matt 5:38-42)? How did Jesus live out his own teachings?

Jesus fed the hungry, comforted the afflicted, cured the sick, healed the blind, treated women with respect

9. a) Treatment of the outcast is addressed in 22:20-23. Who are the "aliens," "widows," and "orphans" in our midst?

migrants, the poor, all without a living wage; the homeless, hungry, those suffering the ravages of war, healed the deaf.

b) How does your parish directly respond to those who may be considered outcasts?

St Vincent de Paul, Lazarus, KfC, Christmas gift donations, food pantry, donations to St Elizabeth's in Haiti, Ukraine

10. a) Why is the sprinkling of blood used to ratify the covenant with God (24:5-8)? (See Lev 17:1-12; Deut 12:23-28.)

Blood is sacred, not to be consumed, but brought to the priest as an offering to God. The splashing of sacrificial blood establishes a community of life between Yahway and His people

b) How is the covenant blood ritual fulfilled in the New Testament? (See Matt 26:27-28; Heb 9:11-28.)

Last Supper and the Eucharistic celebration

CLOSING PRAYER

Prayer

I am the LORD your God, who brought you out of the land of Egypt, out of the house of slavery. You shall not have other gods beside me.

(Exod 20:2-3)

Lord our God, all of your commands, all of your words, and all of your deeds flow from your love for us, your people. Grant that we may recognize your loving presence in all that you ask of us so that we may enjoy the true freedom you desire for us. We pray for those who are searching for you and your liberating presence, especially . . .

LESSON THREE

Exodus 25–31

Begin your personal study and group discussion with a simple and sincere prayer such as:

Prayer

God of the exodus, give us a share in the freedom and life you offer. As we read and study your word, free our minds to understand you and enliven our hearts to love you.

Read the Bible text of Exodus 25–31 found in the outside columns of pages 48–62, highlighting what stands out to you.

Read the accompanying commentary to add to your understanding.

Respond to the questions on pages 63–65, Exploring Lesson Three.

The Closing Prayer on page 66 is for your personal use and may be used at the end of group discussion.

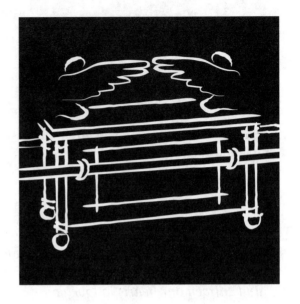

CHAPTER 25

Collection of Materials

[1]The LORD spoke to Moses: [2]Speak to the Israelites: Let them receive contributions for me. From each you shall receive the contribution that their hearts prompt them to give me. [3]These are the contributions you shall accept from them: gold, silver, and bronze; [4]violet, purple, and scarlet yarn; fine linen and goat hair; [5]rams' skins dyed red, and tahash skins; acacia wood; [6]oil for the light; spices for the anointing oil and for the fragrant incense; [7]onyx stones and other gems for mounting on the ephod and the breastpiece. [8]They are to make a sanctuary for me, that I may dwell in their midst. [9]According to all that I show you regarding the pattern of the tabernacle and the pattern of its furnishings, so you are to make it.

continue

25:1-9 Collection of Materials

The people of Israel have moved from servitude to Pharaoh to service of YHWH. Both Israel's servitude and service were expressed in building: the supply cities in Egypt at the beginning of Exodus and the tabernacle for God as the book moves to its conclusion. The first building project was commanded under forced slavery; the tabernacle is built willingly in freedom.

Chapters 25–31 are instructions for building Israel's sanctuary; chapters 35–40 describe the construction of the sanctuary. Such a volume of material focused on the instructions for Israel's tabernacle indicates the importance of worship for the life of the people of Israel. This book of Israel's origins describes Israel's two basic institutions: the law and the sanctuary. Both form Israel's new existence in freedom, giving that life an ethical shape and a liturgical shape.

The final editors of Exodus intend these chapters to be understood within the context of God's further revelation to Moses on the mountain. Now that Israel had entered into covenant, God could reveal the means for continually expressing and experiencing that covenant in worship. Moses is called still further up the mountain to receive instructions for the elements of Israel's ongoing worship as God's people.

The call for material is prefaced by the instruction that all contributions are to be made freely—not compelled—as each one's heart is prompted to give. The materials themselves are some of the finest and rarest available. The metals are listed in descending value, as are the colored yarns made from rare dyes extracted from shellfish and insects.

The purpose of the sanctuary is stated by YHWH: "that I may dwell in their midst." Israel's God will leave the remote mountain, the particular abode for the gods of the ancient Near East, to dwell in the center of human community. The people may have confidence that God dwells there in the midst of the insecurities of the wilderness. The question of God's people at Massah and Meribah, "Is the LORD in our midst or not?" is answered with the assurance that the divine presence can be found in a tangible place that moves along the journey with Israel.

25:10-22 Plan of the Ark

The ark takes first place among the elements of the tabernacle due to its central importance in the whole structure. It is the symbol and vehicle of God's nearness with Israel, serving both as container for the symbols of the covenant and as throne for Yнwн's presence. Its size was unimposing; a cubit represented the distance from one's elbow to fingertips. The opulence of its gold plating and molding suggests its importance as the most sacred object in the tabernacle.

The golden rings and poles emphasize both the mobile character of the ark and its untouchable holiness. The carrying poles are to remain inserted in the rings at all times. The ark is to be carried with the people as they are on the move. It is a reminder of the ongoing journey of God's people and stands over against any attempts to confine God in an immovable abode.

Plan of the Ark

¹⁰You shall make an ark of acacia wood, two and a half cubits long, one and a half cubits wide, and one and a half cubits high. ¹¹Plate it inside and outside with pure gold, and put a molding of gold around the top of it. ¹²Cast four gold rings and put them on the four supports of the ark, two rings on one side and two on the opposite side. ¹³Then make poles of acacia wood and plate them with gold. ¹⁴These poles you are to put through the rings on the sides of the ark, for carrying it; ¹⁵they must remain in the rings of the ark and never be withdrawn. ¹⁶In the ark you are to put the covenant which I will give you.

¹⁷You shall then make a cover of pure gold, two and a half cubits long, and one and a half cubits

continue

The ark of the covenant.

A menorah.

wide. ¹⁸Make two cherubim of beaten gold for the two ends of the cover; ¹⁹make one cherub at one end, and the other at the other end, of one piece with the cover, at each end. ²⁰The cherubim shall have their wings spread out above, sheltering the cover with them; they shall face each other, with their faces looking toward the cover. ²¹This cover you shall then place on top of the ark. In the ark itself you are to put the covenant which I will give you. ²²There I will meet you and there, from above the cover, between the two cherubim on the ark of the covenant, I will tell you all that I command you regarding the Israelites.

The Table

²³You shall also make a table of acacia wood, two cubits long, a cubit wide, and a cubit and a half high. ²⁴Plate it with pure gold and make a molding of gold around it. ²⁵Make a frame for it, a handbreadth high, and make a molding of gold around the frame. ²⁶You shall also make four rings of gold for it and fasten them at the four corners, one at each leg. ²⁷The rings shall be alongside the frame as holders for the poles to carry the table. ²⁸These poles for carrying the table you shall make of acacia wood and plate with gold. ²⁹You shall make its plates and cups, as well as its pitchers and bowls for pouring libations; make them of pure gold. ³⁰On the table you shall always keep show-bread set before me.

The Menorah

³¹You shall make a menorah of pure beaten gold—its shaft and branches—with its cups and knobs and petals springing directly from it. ³²Six branches are to extend from its sides, three branches on one side, and three on the other. ³³On one branch there are to be three cups, shaped like almond blossoms, each with its knob and petals; on the opposite branch there are to be three cups, shaped like almond blossoms, each with its knob and petals; and so for the six

continue

The covering for the ark, made of gold, is the same dimensions as the ark. The cherubim were creatures with human heads but having wings and the body of an animal. They were commonly placed as guardians of thrones and temples in Mesopotamia. According to the Priestly understanding, YHWH's presence was most powerfully experienced above the ark cover and between the cherubim. There Moses would meet God and receive the divine instructions for the people of Israel.

25:23-30 The Table

The table, made from the same material as the ark, was also to be transported with poles. Upon it was to be kept loaves of bread ("showbread"), sometimes translated as "bread of God's presence." Leviticus 24:5-9 describes how the bread and wine were to be placed in the golden vessels. The twelve loaves, to be replaced each Sabbath, were a sacred offering made to YHWH as a pledge of the covenant. The bread offering was accompanied by libations of wine and burning incense on the table. Such a lavish display indicates that the table was a symbol of God's sustaining and nourishing presence with Israel.

25:31-40 The Menorah

The shape of the menorah, made of hammered gold, suggested an almond tree. Its main shaft had three branches growing out of each side. The shaft and six branches were each capped with an open flower design. This same golden blossom was repeated four times along the length of the shaft and three times along each branch. The menorah would hold seven oil lamps at the end of the shaft and each branch.

Functionally, the menorah was to provide light for the tabernacle. Symbolically, its organic pattern suggested the fertility and life that God provides, and the lamps suggested the continual presence of YHWH made known through the constant fire in their midst.

26:1-14 The Tent Cloth

The people of Israel certainly must have had some type of moving tent representing YHWH's presence among them in their Exodus journey. The meeting tent in which Moses communicated with God (33:7ff.) is perhaps the earliest form of this more elaborate tabernacle revealed through Moses on Sinai. Yet how much of the present material is historical and how much is a product of Israel's later construction of sanctuaries and temples is open for speculation.

The tabernacle itself is an elaborate but portable shrine. Many elements of the structure seem unrealistic for a people traveling through the desert. The tabernacle strongly reflects elements of the later temple built by Solomon. It may also reflect earlier elements of the tabernacle at Shiloh (Josh 18:1) and the tent that David built for the ark (2 Sam 6:17). It is both a historical sanctuary and a paradigmatic model for all of Israel's temples.

The tabernacle is described not as a temporary institution but one that will continue through all generations. All the people of Israel

branches that extend from the menorah. [34]On the menorah there are to be four cups, shaped like almond blossoms, with their knobs and petals. [35]The six branches that go out from the menorah are to have a knob under each pair. [36]Their knobs and branches shall so spring from it that the whole will form a single piece of pure beaten gold. [37]You shall then make seven lamps for it and so set up the lamps that they give their light on the space in front of the menorah. [38]These, as well as the trimming shears and trays, must be of pure gold. [39]Use a talent of pure gold for the menorah and all these utensils. [40]See that you make them according to the pattern shown you on the mountain.

CHAPTER 26

The Tent Cloth

[1]The tabernacle itself you shall make out of ten sheets woven of fine linen twined and of violet, purple, and scarlet yarn, with cherubim embroidered on them. [2]The length of each shall be twenty-eight cubits, and the width four cubits; all the sheets shall be of the same size. [3]Five of the sheets are to be joined one to another; and the same for the other five. [4]Make loops of violet yarn along the edge of the end sheet in one set, and the same along the edge of the end sheet in the other set. [5]Make fifty loops along the edge of the end sheet in the first set, and fifty loops along the edge of the corresponding sheet in the second set, and so placed that the loops are directly opposite each other. [6]Then make fifty clasps of gold and join the two sets of sheets, so that the tabernacle forms one whole.

[7]Also make sheets woven of goat hair for a tent over the tabernacle. Make eleven such sheets; [8]the length of each shall be thirty cubits, and the width four cubits: all eleven sheets shall be of the same size. [9]Join five of the sheets into one set, and the other six sheets into another set. Use the sixth sheet double at the front of the tent. [10]Make fifty

continue

loops along the edge of the end sheet in one set, and fifty loops along the edge of the end sheet in the second set. ¹¹Also make fifty bronze clasps and put them into the loops, to join the tent into one whole. ¹²There will be an extra half sheet of tent covering, which shall be allowed to hang down over the rear of the tabernacle. ¹³Likewise, the sheets of the tent will have an extra cubit's length to be left hanging down on either side of the tabernacle to cover it. ¹⁴Over the tent itself make a covering of rams' skins dyed red, and above that, a covering of tahash skins.

The Framework

¹⁵You shall make frames for the tabernacle, acacia-wood uprights. ¹⁶The length of each frame is to be ten cubits, and its width one and a half cubits. ¹⁷Each frame shall have two arms joined one to another; so you are to make all the frames of the tabernacle. ¹⁸Make the frames of the tabernacle as follows: twenty frames on the south side, ¹⁹with forty silver pedestals under the twenty frames, two pedestals under each frame for its two arms; ²⁰twenty frames on the other side of the tabernacle, the north side, ²¹with their forty silver pedestals, two pedestals under each frame. ²²At the rear of the tabernacle, to the west, six frames, ²³and two frames for the corners of the tabernacle, at its rear. ²⁴These two shall be double at the bottom, and likewise double at the top, to the first ring. That is how both corner frames are to be made. ²⁵Thus, there shall be eight frames, with their sixteen silver pedestals, two pedestals under each frame. ²⁶Also make bars of acacia wood: five for the frames on one side of the tabernacle, ²⁷five for those on the other side, and five for those at the rear, to the west. ²⁸The center bar, at the middle of the frames, shall reach across from end to end. ²⁹Plate the frames with gold, and make gold rings on them as holders for the bars, which are also to be plated with gold. ³⁰You shall set up the tabernacle according to its plan, which you were shown on the mountain.

continue

continue to experience through time both the law and the sanctuary revealed on Sinai. Just as the law has a foundational form but includes variations and adaptions throughout history, so the basic structure of Israel's worship has a foundation with modifications and adjustments made throughout history.

Since the Priestly tradition was edited during the time of the exile, the writers are looking back through the days of the glorious temple of Solomon to the desert sanctuary, and they are looking forward to the future rebuilding of the temple after their exile. Through reading the text, a majestic sanctuary is summoned in the mind through memory of the past and hope for the future. The sanctuary thus evoked unites the people of Israel in every age with their worshiping ancestors throughout history.

The network of tapestries that comprise the inner part of the structure are made of fine linen and dyed yarns and the two halves are held together with fifty golden clasps. Cherubim are embroidered on the linen sheets that could be seen from inside the structure. Over this inner lining were placed sheets made of goat hair that hung a cubit longer on each side to cover the tapestry. Finally, two outer coverings of animal skins protected the structure from the elements.

26:15-30 The Framework

The cloth was supported by a series of upright frames made of acacia wood set into silver pedestals. The supports were strengthened by crossbars to be held in place by gold rings attached to the upright frames. The frame formed a rectangular structure, with upright supports on three sides, with two specially constructed corner supports, and open to the east.

Though described in some detail, there are many uncertainties about the construction. Our understanding of Hebrew technical terms like "frames," "arms," "pedestals," and "bars" is incomplete. The structure was designed to facilitate portability, so that the entire structure could be transported and reassembled in a short period of time.

26:31-37 The Veils

A veil made of fine linen and embroidered with cherubim divided the tabernacle into two sections: the larger holy place and the "holy of holies." The ark of the covenant was to be placed behind the veil in the "holy of holies." The table with showbread and the menorah were to be placed outside the veil, opposite each other in the holy place. The open east end of the tabernacle was to be closed by a curtain, made of the same material as the inner veil but embroidered in multicolored patterns.

27:1-8 The Altar for Burnt Offerings

An altar for offering animal sacrifices was to be made of acacia and overlaid with bronze. The altar was to have horn-like projections at each of its four corners. Various utensils for the sacrifices were also to be made of bronze. A grate was to be used presumably to hold the fire and the offering while allowing the ashes and grease to fall below. The whole construction was to be hollow for easier transport.

27:9-19 Court of the Tabernacle

The courtyard was to surround the sanctuary and separate the activities of worship from the world outside. The court was enclosed by hangings of fine linen stretched between a series of sixty columns set in bronze pedestals. The entrance on the east was to be covered with a screen made of the same material and pattern as the screen covering the entrance to the holy place. The court was considered as part of the tabernacle, the area where public ceremonies took place.

27:20-21 Oil for the Lamps

The oil used in the lampstand was to be provided by the people of Israel and tended by the priests. It was to be the purest form of olive oil, extracted by hand rather than pressed, as is fitting for the place of its use. Such oil gives a bright, clean light with little smoke. The lamps are always to be kept burning throughout the night in front of the holy of holies from generation to generation.

The Veils

31You shall make a veil woven of violet, purple, and scarlet yarn, and of fine linen twined, with cherubim embroidered on it. 32It is to be hung on four gold-plated columns of acacia wood, which shall have gold hooks and shall rest on four silver pedestals. 33Hang the veil from clasps. The ark of the covenant you shall bring inside, behind this veil which divides the holy place from the holy of holies. 34Set the cover on the ark of the covenant in the holy of holies.

35Outside the veil you shall place the table and the menorah, the latter on the south side of the tabernacle, opposite the table, which is to be put on the north side. 36For the entrance of the tent make a variegated curtain of violet, purple, and scarlet yarn and of fine linen twined. 37Make five columns of acacia wood for this curtain; plate them with gold, with their hooks of gold; and cast five bronze pedestals for them.

CHAPTER 27

The Altar for Burnt Offerings

1You shall make an altar of acacia wood, on a square, five cubits long and five cubits wide; it shall be three cubits high. 2At the four corners make horns that are of one piece with the altar. You shall then plate it with bronze. 3Make pots for removing the ashes, as well as shovels, basins, forks, and fire pans; all these utensils you shall make of bronze. 4Make for it a grating, a bronze network; make four bronze rings for it, one at each of its four corners. 5Put it down around the altar, on the ground. This network is to be half as high as the altar. 6You shall also make poles of acacia wood for the altar, and plate them with bronze. 7These poles are to be put through the rings, so that they are on either side of the altar when it is carried. 8Make the altar itself in the form of a hollow box. Just as it was shown you on the mountain, so it is to be made.

continue

Court of the Tabernacle

⁹You shall also make a court for the tabernacle. On the south side the court shall have hangings, of fine linen twined, a hundred cubits long, ¹⁰with twenty columns and twenty pedestals of bronze; the hooks and bands on the columns shall be of silver. ¹¹On the north side there shall be similar hangings, a hundred cubits long, with twenty columns and twenty pedestals of bronze; the hooks and bands on the columns shall be of silver. ¹²On the west side, across the width of the court, there shall be hangings, fifty cubits long, with ten columns and ten pedestals. ¹³The width of the court on the east side shall be fifty cubits. ¹⁴On one side there shall be hangings to the extent of fifteen cubits, with three columns and three pedestals; ¹⁵on the other side there shall be hangings to the extent of fifteen cubits, with three columns and three pedestals.

¹⁶At the gate of the court there shall be a variegated curtain, twenty cubits long, woven of violet, purple, and scarlet yarn and of fine linen twined. It shall have four columns and four pedestals.

¹⁷All the columns around the court shall have bands and hooks of silver, and pedestals of bronze. ¹⁸The court is to be one hundred cubits long, fifty cubits wide, and five cubits high. Fine linen twined must be used, and the pedestals must be of bronze. ¹⁹All the fittings of the tabernacle, whatever be their use, as well as all its tent pegs and all the tent pegs of the court, must be of bronze.

Oil for the Lamps

²⁰You shall command the Israelites to bring you clear oil of crushed olives, to be used for the light, so that you may keep lamps burning always. ²¹From evening to morning Aaron and his sons shall maintain them before the LORD in the tent of meeting, outside the veil which hangs in front of the covenant. This shall be a perpetual statute for the Israelites throughout their generations.

CHAPTER 28

The Priestly Vestments

¹Have your brother Aaron, and with him his sons, brought to you, from among the Israelites, that they may be my priests: Nadab and Abihu, Eleazar and Ithamar, Aaron's sons. ²For the glorious adornment of your brother Aaron you shall have sacred vestments made. ³Therefore, tell the various artisans whom I have endowed with skill to make vestments for Aaron to consecrate him as my priest. ⁴These are the vestments they shall make: a breastpiece, an ephod, a robe, a brocade tunic, a turban, and a sash. In making these sacred vestments which your brother Aaron and his sons are to wear in serving as my priests, ⁵they shall use gold, violet, purple, and scarlet yarn and fine linen.

The Ephod and Breastpiece

⁶The ephod they shall make of gold thread and of violet, purple, and scarlet yarn, embroidered on cloth of fine linen twined. ⁷It shall have a pair of shoulder straps joined to its two upper ends. ⁸The embroidered belt of the ephod shall extend out from it and, like it, be made of gold thread, of violet, purple, and scarlet yarn, and of fine linen twined.

⁹Get two onyx stones and engrave on them the names of the sons of Israel: ¹⁰six of their names on one stone, and the names of the remaining six on the other stone, in the order of their birth. ¹¹As a gem-cutter engraves a seal, so shall you have the two stones engraved with the names of the sons of Israel and then mounted in gold filigree work. ¹²Set these two stones on the shoulder straps of the ephod as memorial stones of the sons of Israel. Thus Aaron shall bear their names on his shoulders as a reminder before the LORD. ¹³Make filigree rosettes of gold, ¹⁴as well as two chains of pure gold, twisted like cords, and fasten the cord-like chains to the filigree rosettes.

¹⁵The breastpiece of decision you shall also have made, embroidered like the ephod with gold

continue

28:1-5 The Priestly Vestments

With the description of the tabernacle complete, the text now turns to the priesthood of Israel who will minister within it. The priesthood became a hereditary office with priests tracing their ancestry to Aaron. As mediators between YHWH and Israel, the priests presented sacrifices to God, made legal decisions about God's will, pronounced blessings upon the people, and tended to the sacred services within the tabernacle.

The wardrobe described here represents an evolution of design as the vestments developed through the centuries. It is probable that some of the elaborate vestments described here were originally worn by the kings of Israel as they performed their sacred duties as YHWH's anointed ones. They were later adapted for priestly use, especially after the demise of the monarchy during the time of the exile.

The focus of the text is on the vestments of Aaron, the high priest. They are to be made for "glorious adornment" by artists specially endowed by YHWH. Made from the same splendid materials as the sanctuary, the vestments matched the grandeur of the place in which the priest ministered and they set the priest apart for sacred service.

28:6-30 The Ephod and Breastpiece

The "ephod" is a garment, the function of which is not fully known. It seems to be a kind of apron or vest with a decorated belt around the waist. The shoulder pieces are designed to hold up the garment and to provide the setting for the two engraved onyx stones. Bearing the names of the twelve sons of Israel, these stones served as symbolic reminders that the priest represented all the people of Israel in the presence of God.

The "breastpiece of decision" was a square pouch, the span of a hand in length and width, woven with the same material as the ephod. On it were mounted four rows of three gemstones each, engraved with the names of the twelve tribes of Israel. A system of golden rings and gold and violet cords attached the breastpiece firmly to the shoulder pieces and the ephod so that it would lie close to the chest.

thread and violet, purple, and scarlet yarn on cloth of fine linen twined. [16]It is to be square when folded double, a span high and a span wide. [17]On it you shall mount four rows of precious stones: in the first row, a carnelian, a topaz, and an emerald; [18]in the second row, a garnet, a sapphire, and a beryl; [19]in the third row, a jacinth, an agate, and an amethyst; [20]in the fourth row, a chrysolite, an onyx, and a jasper. These stones are to be mounted in gold filigree work, [21]twelve of them to match the names of the sons of Israel, each stone engraved like a seal with the name of one of the twelve tribes.

[22]When the chains of pure gold, twisted like cords, have been made for the breastpiece, [23]you shall then make two rings of gold for it and fasten them to the two upper ends of the breastpiece. [24]The gold cords are then to be fastened to the two rings at the upper ends of the breastpiece, [25]the other two ends of the cords being fastened in front to the two filigree rosettes which are attached to the shoulder straps of the ephod. [26]Make two other rings of gold and put them on the two lower ends of the breastpiece, on its edge that faces the ephod. [27]Then make two more rings of gold and fasten them to the bottom of the shoulder straps next to where they join the ephod in front, just above its embroidered belt. [28]Violet ribbons shall bind the rings of the breastpiece to the rings of the ephod, so that the breastpiece will stay right above the embroidered belt of the ephod and not swing loose from it.

continue

The "Urim and Thummim" were an oracular device kept within the breastpiece and used by the high priest for interpreting the decisions of YHWH. How the message of YHWH was made known through them is uncertain (1 Sam 14:41). Verses 29-30 three times repeat the phrases "over Aaron's/his heart" and "the presence of YHWH." Aaron holds the people of Israel close to his heart when he enters the sanctuary to worship or to discern the decisions of YHWH for them.

²⁹Whenever Aaron enters the sanctuary, he will thus bear the names of the sons of Israel on the breastpiece of decision over his heart as a constant reminder before the LORD. ³⁰In this breastpiece of decision you shall put the Urim and Thummim, that they may be over Aaron's heart whenever he enters the presence of the LORD. Thus he shall always bear the decisions for the Israelites over his heart in the presence of the LORD.

Other Vestments

³¹The robe of the ephod you shall make entirely of violet material. ³²It shall have an opening for the head in the center, and around this opening there shall be a selvage, woven as at the opening of a shirt, to keep it from being torn. ³³At the hem at the bottom you shall make pomegranates, woven of violet, purple, and scarlet yarn and fine linen twined, with gold bells between them; ³⁴a gold bell, a pomegranate, a gold bell, a pomegranate, all around the hem of the robe. ³⁵Aaron shall wear it when ministering, that its sound may be heard as he enters and leaves the LORD's presence in the sanctuary; else he will die.

³⁶You shall also make a plate of pure gold and engrave on it, as on a seal engraving, "Sacred to the LORD." ³⁷This plate is to be tied over the turban with a violet ribbon in such a way that it rests on the front of the turban, ³⁸over Aaron's forehead. Since Aaron bears whatever guilt the Israelites may incur in consecrating any of their sacred gifts, this plate must always be over his forehead, so that they may find favor with the LORD.

³⁹The tunic of fine linen shall be brocaded. The turban shall be made of fine linen. The sash shall be of variegated work.

⁴⁰Likewise, for the glorious adornment of Aaron's sons you shall have tunics and sashes and skullcaps made, for glorious splendor. ⁴¹With these you shall clothe your brother Aaron and his sons. Anoint and install them, consecrating them as my priests. ⁴²You must also make linen pants for them, to cover their naked flesh from their

continue

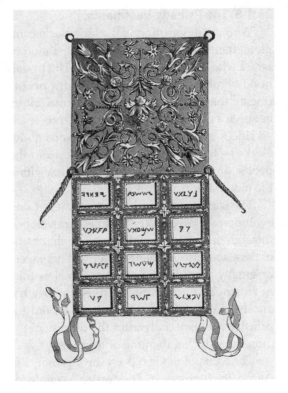

Breastpiece of decision described in Exodus 28.

28:31-43 Other Vestments

Under the ephod and breastpiece the high priest was to wear a violet robe. This was a sleeveless garment made of one piece with an opening for slipping it on over the head. Alternating around the bottom of the robe were pomegranates and golden bells. Pomegranates were common symbols of fertility and life. The bells could be heard tinkling as an announcement of entry into YHWH's presence. They would be heard by the people outside during the sacred ceremonies so that they would know the priest is still alive before the awesome divine presence.

The engraved plate, to be placed on the front of the turban, signified that the high priest was set apart for God's service. It further indicated that all Israel, whom Aaron represented in God's presence, was sacred to YHWH. Though the high priest bore the guilt of Israel upon himself, the plate symbolized that God continues to redeem the chosen people.

The tunic was a long shirt-like garment worn under the robe. The sash was wrapped around the tunic at the waist. The turban was a ceremonial headgear made of linen wrapped around the head. The vestments of the other priests were simpler, consisting of tunics, sashes, and less elaborate skullcaps. Vesting in sacred garments was part of the first stage in the ritual of consecration for Israel's priesthood.

29:1-9 Consecration of the Priests

The text moves from a description of priestly vestments to the ritual of priestly ordination. It is assumed that Moses himself will make the preparations and perform the rites for Aaron and his sons. "Consecrate" means to set apart for divine service. The ritual reflects elements that were added through the centuries down to the ritual performed by the Priestly tradition after the exile.

The first stage of the ritual is carried out in several parts. First, all the sacrificial animals and the cereal offerings are brought to the entrance of the tent along with Aaron and his sons. Second, those to be ordained are ritually washed as a sign of purification, probably at the bronze basin described in 30:17ff. Third, they are ceremonially vested with the garments symbolizing their office. Fourth, the anointing oil (30:22ff.) is poured over the heads of those being ordained.

29:10-46 Installation Sacrifices

The ordination is consummated by a series of three types of sacrificial offerings. Before each sacrifice Aaron and his sons were to place their hands on the head of the animal, symbolizing their identification with it. The young bull was to be sacrificed as a purification offering. Some of its blood was placed on the horns of the altar to purify it and the rest of the blood poured out at the altar's base. The bull was to be completely burned, both on the altar and outside the camp, securing forgiveness of sins for those being ordained.

One of the rams was then sacrificed as a whole burnt offering. After its blood was

loins to their thighs. [43]Aaron and his sons shall wear them whenever they go into the tent of meeting or approach the altar to minister in the sanctuary, lest they incur guilt and die. This shall be a perpetual ordinance for him and for his descendants.

CHAPTER 29

Consecration of the Priests

[1]This is the rite you shall perform in consecrating them as my priests. Procure a young bull and two unblemished rams. [2]With bran flour make unleavened cakes mixed with oil, and unleavened wafers spread with oil, [3]and put them in a basket. Take the basket of them along with the bull and the two rams. [4]Aaron and his sons you shall also bring to the entrance of the tent of meeting, and there wash them with water. [5]Take the vestments and clothe Aaron with the tunic, the robe of the ephod, the ephod itself, and the breastpiece, fastening the embroidered belt of the ephod around him. [6]Put the turban on his head, the sacred diadem on the turban. [7]Then take the anointing oil and pour it on his head, and anoint him. [8]Bring forward his sons also and clothe them with the tunics, [9]gird them with the sashes, and tie the skullcaps on them. Thus shall the priesthood be theirs by a perpetual statute, and thus shall you install Aaron and his sons.

Installation Sacrifices

[10]Now bring forward the bull in front of the tent of meeting. There Aaron and his sons shall lay their hands on its head. [11]Then slaughter the bull before the LORD, at the entrance of the tent of meeting. [12]Take some of its blood and with your finger put it on the horns of the altar. All the rest of the blood you shall pour out at the base of the altar. [13]All the fat that covers its inner organs, as well as the lobe of its liver and its two kidneys, together with the fat that is on them, you shall take and burn on the altar. [14]But the meat and

continue

hide and dung of the bull you must burn up outside the camp, since this is a purification offering.

¹⁵Then take one of the rams, and after Aaron and his sons have laid their hands on its head, ¹⁶slaughter it. The blood you shall take and splash on all the sides of the altar. ¹⁷Cut the ram into pieces; you shall wash its inner organs and shanks and put them with the pieces and with the head. ¹⁸Then you shall burn the entire ram on the altar, since it is a burnt offering, a sweet-smelling oblation to the LORD.

¹⁹After this take the other ram, and when Aaron and his sons have laid their hands on its head, ²⁰slaughter it. Some of its blood you shall take and put on the tip of Aaron's right ear and on the tips of his sons' right ears and on the thumbs of their right hands and the great toes of their right feet. Splash the rest of the blood on all the sides of the altar. ²¹Then take some of the blood that is on the altar, together with some of the anointing oil, and sprinkle this on Aaron and his vestments, as well as on his sons and their vestments, that he and his sons and their vestments may be sacred.

²²Now, from this ram you shall take its fat: its fatty tail, the fat that covers its inner organs, the lobe of its liver, its two kidneys with the fat that is on them, and its right thigh, since this is the ram for installation; ²³then, out of the basket of unleavened food that you have set before the LORD, you shall take one of the loaves of bread, one of the cakes made with oil, and one of the wafers. ²⁴All these things you shall put into the hands of Aaron and his sons, so that they may raise them as an elevated offering before the LORD. ²⁵After you receive them back from their hands, you shall burn them on top of the burnt offering on the altar as a sweet-smelling oblation to the LORD. ²⁶Finally, take the brisket of Aaron's installation ram and raise it as an elevated offering before the LORD; this is to be your own portion.

²⁷Thus shall you set aside the brisket of whatever elevated offering is raised, as well as the thigh of whatever contribution is raised up, whether this be the installation ram or anything else belonging to Aaron or to his sons. ²⁸Such things are due to Aaron and his sons from the Israelites by a perpetual statute as a contribution. From their communion offerings, too, the Israelites shall make a contribution, their contribution to the LORD.

²⁹The sacred vestments of Aaron shall be passed down to his sons after him, that in them they may be anointed and installed. ³⁰The son who succeeds him as priest and who is to enter the tent of meeting to minister in the sanctuary shall be clothed with them for seven days.

³¹You shall take the installation ram and boil its meat in a holy place. ³²At the entrance of the tent of meeting Aaron and his sons shall eat the meat of the ram and the bread that is in the basket. ³³They themselves are to eat of these things by which atonement was made at their installation and consecration; but no unauthorized person may eat of them, since they are sacred. ³⁴If some of the meat of the installation sacrifice or some of the bread remains over on the next day, this remnant you must burn up; it is not to be eaten, since it is sacred.

³⁵Carry out all these commands in regard to Aaron and his sons just as I have given them to you. Seven days you shall spend installing them, ³⁶sacrificing a bull each day as a purification offering, to make atonement. Thus you shall purify the altar by purging it, and you shall anoint it in order to consecrate it. ³⁷Seven days you shall spend in purging the altar and in consecrating it. Then the altar will be most sacred, and whatever touches it will become sacred.

³⁸Now, this is what you shall regularly offer on the altar: two yearling lambs as the sacrifice established for each day; ³⁹one lamb in the morning and the other lamb at the evening twilight. ⁴⁰With the first lamb there shall be a tenth of an ephah of bran flour mixed with a fourth of a hin of oil of crushed olives and, as its libation, a fourth of a hin of wine. ⁴¹The other lamb you shall offer at the evening twilight, with the same grain offering and libation as in the morning. You shall offer

continue

splashed around the altar, its inner organs were washed and the whole animal burned on the altar. The second ram was then sacrificed as a communion offering. Its blood was to be put on the extremities of the priests' right ears, hands, and feet, representing the purification of their entire body. Then the blood and anointing oil were to be sprinkled on the priests and their vestments, setting them apart for sacred ministry. Specified parts of the ram along with selected offerings of unleavened bread were to be placed in the hands of the priests and elevated from the altar as a sign of dedication to God. Part of the sacrifice was burned on the altar, and then the breast and thigh were given as food for the priests. They were to be boiled and then eaten with the remaining bread at the entrance to the tent.

The altar must also be cleansed with the purification offering and anointed. Its consecration will enable the altar to be used for special ceremonial sacrifices as well as the daily sacrifices to Yhwh. Every morning and every evening a lamb is to be sacrificed along with an offering of flour, oil, and wine. Thus, the opening and closing of every day would be marked with offerings to God throughout every generation.

Verses 44-46 summarize the previous chapters concerning the tabernacle. God's meeting with the people of Israel makes holy the tent, the altar, and the priests. The very God who brought them out of Egypt continues to dwell among them. The purpose of Israel's institutions of worship is to enable Israel to continue to experience the life-giving presence of their liberating God.

30:1-10 Altar of Incense

The instructions for the altar of incense are not given where we would expect, with the instructions for the ark, the table, and the menorah. Like them, it is to be made of acacia wood and plated with gold. Like them, it is to be placed in the holy place but ready for movement with its golden carrying poles.

The altar is to be placed in front of the veil, apparently between the table and the menorah.

this as a sweet-smelling oblation to the Lord. [42]Throughout your generations this regular burnt offering shall be made before the Lord at the entrance of the tent of meeting, where I will meet you and speak to you.

[43]There, at the altar, I will meet the Israelites; hence, it will be made sacred by my glory. [44]Thus I will consecrate the tent of meeting and the altar, just as I also consecrate Aaron and his sons to be my priests. [45]I will dwell in the midst of the Israelites and will be their God. [46]They shall know that I, the Lord, am their God who brought them out of the land of Egypt, so that I, the Lord, their God, might dwell among them.

CHAPTER 30

Altar of Incense

[1]For burning incense you shall make an altar of acacia wood, [2]with a square surface, a cubit long, a cubit wide, and two cubits high, with horns that are of one piece with it. [3]Its grate on top, its walls on all four sides, and its horns you shall plate with pure gold. Put a gold molding around it. [4]Underneath the molding you shall put gold rings, two on one side and two on the opposite side, as holders for the poles used in carrying it. [5]Make the poles, too, of acacia wood and plate them with gold. [6]This altar you are to place in front of the veil that hangs before the ark of the covenant where I will meet you.

[7]On it Aaron shall burn fragrant incense. Morning after morning, when he prepares the lamps, [8]and again in the evening twilight, when he lights the lamps, he shall burn incense. Throughout your generations this shall be the regular incense offering before the Lord. [9]On this altar you shall not offer up any profane incense, or any burnt offering or grain offering; nor shall you pour out a libation upon it. [10]Once a year Aaron shall purge its horns. Throughout your generations he is to purge it once a year with the blood of the atoning purification offering. This altar is most sacred to the Lord.

continue

Census Tax

[11]The LORD also told Moses: [12]When you take a census of the Israelites who are to be enrolled, each one, as he is enrolled, shall give the LORD a ransom for his life, so that no plague may come upon them for being enrolled. [13]This is what everyone who is enrolled must pay: a half-shekel, according to the standard of the sanctuary shekel—twenty gerahs to the shekel—a half-shekel contribution to the LORD. [14]Everyone who is enrolled, of twenty years or more, must give the contribution to the LORD. [15]The rich need not give more, nor shall the poor give less, than a half-shekel in this contribution to the LORD to pay the ransom for their lives. [16]When you receive this ransom money from the Israelites, you shall donate it to the service of the tent of meeting, that there it may be a reminder of the Israelites before the LORD of the ransom paid for their lives.

The Basin

[17]The LORD told Moses: [18]For ablutions you shall make a bronze basin with a bronze stand. Place it between the tent of meeting and the altar, and put water in it. [19]Aaron and his sons shall use it in washing their hands and feet. [20]When they are about to enter the tent of meeting, they must wash with water, lest they die. Likewise when they approach the altar to minister, to offer an oblation to the LORD, [21]they must wash their hands and feet, lest they die. This shall be a perpetual statute for him and his descendants throughout their generations.

The Anointing Oil

[22]The LORD told Moses: [23]Take the finest spices: five hundred shekels of free-flowing myrrh; half that amount, that is, two hundred and fifty shekels, of fragrant cinnamon; two hundred and fifty shekels of fragrant cane; [24]five hundred shekels of cassia—all according to the standard of the sanctuary shekel; together with a hin of olive oil; [25]and blend them into sacred anointing

continue

Incense must be burned on the altar twice daily, near the time of the sacrifices. Only the type of incense prescribed in verses 34ff. may be used and no other types of offering may be made on this altar. The altar is to be purified each year on the Day of Atonement by putting the blood of the purification offering on the horns of the altar.

30:11-16 Census Tax

Chapters 30–31 seem to be supplementary to the bulk of instructions that have preceded them. The directions contained in these chapters, though related thematically to the tabernacle, are not as closely joined as the previous chapters. The supplementary nature of these sections is indicated by the introductory phrase, "The LORD (also) told Moses" (30:11, 17, 22, 34; 31:1, 12), which interrupts the lengthy sequence of divine instructions that precedes them. Their subject matter is miscellaneous and their sequence is somewhat arbitrary. However, they are all connected to Israel's worship and were judged to be important by those responsible for editing the traditions of Israel.

Why the taking of a census was considered dangerous is uncertain. Yet the practice is included here because it provided the financial support for Israel's sanctuary. Each one who registered, twenty years or older, must pay a half shekel as a "ransom" to preserve him from harm. The instruction that everyone should pay the same amount, rich and poor alike, indicates the equality with which each Israelite would be a "reminder" before YHWH. An earlier system of counting and taxation that provoked fear probably became, in time, a means of being united with the worship of Israel and remembered by YHWH.

30:17-21 The Basin

The laver of bronze, used for ritual washing, was to be placed in the courtyard of the tabernacle between the tent and the altar of sacrifice. The priests would cleanse their hands and feet before they entered the tent of meeting or before they offered sacrifice on the altar. The threat of death for not paying the half shekel and for not washing emphasizes the close connection between Israel's worship of Yʜᴡʜ and the gift of life given to each person by Yʜᴡʜ.

30:22-33 The Anointing Oil

The specially blended oil, made from aromatic ingredients and a gallon of olive oil, was to be used for the anointing of the tent and all the furnishings and implements of the tent and the court. It is also the anointing oil with which the priests were to be consecrated. Besides setting them apart for sacred functions, the oil also carried connotations of vitality and life. The anointed one was given vitality that was characteristic of the living God and received a share in the life of Yʜᴡʜ. The various rituals of the tabernacle made use of blood, water, or oil—all symbols of participation in God's life.

30:34-38 The Incense

Similarly unique and restricted to use in divine worship, the incense was to be burned on the golden altar of incense. Various spices and resins combined to provide a pleasing fragrance and a mysterious smokiness reminiscent of Yʜᴡʜ's presence in fire and cloud.

31:1-11 Choice of Artisans

Since God has specified that the materials for the creation of the tabernacle should be the finest, it is appropriate that the artistry by which the tabernacle was created should also be the best. The choice of Bezalel as the managing artisan for the construction of God's tabernacle and of his assistant and other workers seems to be a logical conclusion to the long catalog of instructions that have preceded. It affords an opportunity to review all the furnishings, vestments, and supplies that they are charged with creating.

There is a marked contrast between the dignity associated with work done in freedom and the brutal labor of slavery. There is pride and concern associated with mastery in the art of embroidery, metalwork, jewelry, and wood carving. God's spirit is recognized as the source of the artisan's skill, talent, and competence.

oil, perfumed ointment expertly prepared. With this sacred anointing oil [26]you shall anoint the tent of meeting and the ark of the covenant, [27]the table and all its utensils, the menorah and its utensils, the altar of incense [28]and the altar for burnt offerings with all its utensils, and the basin with its stand. [29]When you have consecrated them, they shall be most sacred; whatever touches them shall be sacred. [30]Aaron and his sons you shall also anoint and consecrate as my priests. [31]Tell the Israelites: As sacred anointing oil this shall belong to me throughout your generations. [32]It may not be used in any ordinary anointing of the body, nor may you make any other oil of a like mixture. It is sacred, and shall be treated as sacred by you. [33]Whoever prepares a perfume like this, or whoever puts any of this on an unauthorized person, shall be cut off from his people.

The Incense

[34]The Lᴏʀᴅ told Moses: Take these aromatic substances: storax and onycha and galbanum, these and pure frankincense in equal parts; [35]and blend them into incense. This fragrant powder, expertly prepared, is to be salted and so kept pure and sacred. [36]Grind some of it into fine dust and put this before the covenant in the tent of meeting where I will meet you. This incense shall be treated as most sacred by you. [37]You may not make incense of a like mixture for yourselves; you must treat it as sacred to the Lᴏʀᴅ. [38]Whoever makes an incense like this for his own enjoyment of its fragrance, shall be cut off from his people.

CHAPTER 31

Choice of Artisans

[1]The Lᴏʀᴅ said to Moses: [2]See, I have singled out Bezalel, son of Uri, son of Hur, of the tribe of Judah, [3]and I have filled him with a divine spirit of skill and understanding and knowledge in every craft: [4]in the production of embroidery, in making things of gold, silver, or bronze, [5]in cutting and mounting precious stones, in carving wood, and

continue

in every other craft. ⁶As his assistant I myself have appointed Oholiab, son of Ahisamach, of the tribe of Dan. I have also endowed all the experts with the necessary skill to make all the things I have commanded you: ⁷the tent of meeting, the ark of the covenant with its cover, all the furnishings of the tent, ⁸the table with its utensils, the pure gold menorah with all its utensils, the altar of incense, ⁹the altar for burnt offerings with all its utensils, the basin with its stand, ¹⁰the service cloths, the sacred vestments for Aaron the priest, the vestments for his sons in their ministry, ¹¹the anointing oil, and the fragrant incense for the sanctuary. According to all I have commanded you, so shall they do.

Sabbath Laws

¹²The LORD said to Moses: ¹³You must also tell the Israelites: Keep my sabbaths, for that is to be the sign between you and me throughout the generations, to show that it is I, the LORD, who make you holy. ¹⁴Therefore, you must keep the sabbath for it is holiness for you. Whoever desecrates it shall be put to death. If anyone does work on that day, that person must be cut off from the people. ¹⁵Six days there are for doing work, but the seventh day is the sabbath of complete rest, holy to the LORD. Anyone who does work on the sabbath day shall be put to death. ¹⁶So shall the Israelites observe the sabbath, keeping it throughout their generations as an everlasting covenant. ¹⁷Between me and the Israelites it is to be an everlasting sign; for in six days the LORD made the heavens and the earth, but on the seventh day he rested at his ease.

¹⁸When the LORD had finished speaking to Moses on Mount Sinai, he gave him the two tablets of the covenant, the stone tablets inscribed by God's own finger.

31:12-18 Sabbath Laws

The instructions to observe the Sabbath serve as a conclusion to this section concerning the tabernacle. Having given directions for its construction and appointed workers for the task, YHWH commands that all this work is to be done according to the six-day rhythm established by God's law. The Sabbath laws also conclude the establishment of the covenant on Sinai begun in chapter 19. The Sabbath is the sign of the covenant by which Israel was to be YHWH's "treasured possession . . . a kingdom of priests, a holy nation" (19:5-6). By obeying the Sabbath the people of Israel would perpetually show that they are set apart, made "holy" by God (v. 13).

This observance of the Sabbath unites Israel with the rhythm of life as it was established by God. As God created the world in six days and rested on the seventh, so Israel was to create the tabernacle of YHWH and continue to live in God's covenant marked by this weekly sign. The penalty of death associated with violation of the Sabbath again emphasizes the Sabbath's close relationship to life as YHWH designed it. Disregard for the Sabbath is disregard for God who saved Israel from death and chose her to experience life in its fullness.

The two tablets of the commandments (31:18) contained the "ten words," a concrete summary of God's covenant with Israel. God's gift of the tablets fulfilled what had been promised as Moses ascended the mountain (24:12). The inclusion formed by this promise and its fulfillment, into which the Priestly material concerning Israel's worship has been inserted, links the ethical law and the liturgical law of Israel. Likewise, the command to place the tablets in the ark of the covenant (25:16) binds the laws of Israel closely to their worship. In fact, the first legal obligation of this covenanted people was to worship their God.

EXPLORING LESSON THREE

1. All members of the community contribute to building the tabernacle for Yhwh (25:1-8), giving as "their hearts prompt them" (25:2). Why do you think Yhwh requests this, and what relevance does it have for our own worshiping communities?

Yhwh wanted His people to be touched with a sense of belonging to this covenented community by participating materially in the construction of the tabernacle ✓

2. Why is the ark of the covenant so precious to Israel (25:8-22)? (See 2 Sam 6:11-15.)

It will carry the Ten Commandments and be with them all through their wandering in the desert.

3. Why is Mary sometimes called the new ark of the covenant? (See Luke 1:35-45.)

4. a) Describe a time when the physical environment enhanced your experience of worship.

   b) In your mind's eye, look around your parish church. What message is being communicated to the congregation by the physical structure and environment that is found there?

5. Considering that such care was given to every element of the wilderness tabernacle, do you have a greater appreciation of what it means to be part of God's dwelling yourself? (See 1 Cor 6:19-20; Eph 2:19-22; 1 Pet 2:4-5.)

_____

_____

_____

_____

_____

6. Why would the instruments of decision-making or discernment be worn over the heart (28:29-30)? (See Lev 8:7-8; Sir 45:10-11.)

_____

_____

_____

_____

_____

_____

7. a) On what sorts of occasions in the Bible was oil used for anointing? (See 29:7; 30:26-32; 1 Sam 10:1; Mark 6:13; John 12:1-8; Jas 5:14.)

_____

_____

_____

_____

b) When is anointing oil used in the church today?

_____

_____

_____

_____

8. Even after all the sacrifices from the priests, what truly makes the tabernacle sacred (29:43)?

_____

_____

_____

_____

9. How does the construction of the tabernacle (31:1-11) differ from Israel's earlier works of construction in Egypt? (See 1:11-14; 5:14-21.)

_____

_____

_____

_____

_____

10. a) Commands concerning the Sabbath have been repeated often (20:8-11; 23:12; 31:12-17). Why do you think there is such a strong emphasis on this command?

_____

_____

_____

_____

b) What relevance does the Sabbath (observed on Sunday by Christians) have for us today? How do we set this day aside as holy?

_____

_____

_____

_____

CLOSING PRAYER

Prayer

I will dwell in the midst of the Israelites and will be their God. They shall know that I, the LORD, am their God who brought them out of the land of Egypt, so that I, the LORD, their God, might dwell among them. (Exod 29:45-46)

Lord God, you were with your people on every step of their desert journey. Be with us as we journey through life. Guide our steps and show us the right path. Give us assurance of your presence among us, and may you dwell forever in the tabernacle of our hearts. We pray today for those who have lost their way or who need assurance of your presence, especially . . .

LESSON FOUR

Exodus 32–40

Begin your personal study and group discussion with a simple and sincere prayer such as:

Prayer

God of the exodus, give us a share in the freedom and life you offer. As we read and study your word, free our minds to understand you and enliven our hearts to love you.

Read the Bible text of Exodus 32–40 found in the outside columns of pages 68–85, highlighting what stands out to you.

Read the accompanying commentary to add to your understanding.

Respond to the questions on pages 87–89, Exploring Lesson Four.

The Closing Prayer on page 90 is for your personal use and may be used at the end of group discussion.

VII. Israel's Apostasy and God's Renewal of the Covenant

CHAPTER 32

The Golden Calf

[1] When the people saw that Moses was delayed in coming down from the mountain, they gathered around Aaron and said to him, "Come, make us a god who will go before us; as for that man Moses who brought us out of the land of Egypt, we do not know what has happened to him." [2] Aaron replied, "Take off the golden earrings that your wives, your sons, and your daughters are wearing, and bring them to me." [3] So all the people took off their earrings and brought them to Aaron. [4] He received their offering, and fashioning it with a tool, made a molten calf. Then they cried out, "These are your gods, Israel, who brought you up from the land of Egypt." [5] On seeing this, Aaron built an altar in front of the calf and proclaimed, "Tomorrow is a feast of the LORD." [6] Early the next day the people sacrificed burnt offerings and brought communion sacrifices. Then they sat down to eat and drink, and rose up to revel.

[7] Then the LORD said to Moses: Go down at once because your people, whom you brought out of the land of Egypt, have acted corruptly. [8] They have quickly turned aside from the way I commanded them, making for themselves a molten calf and bowing down to it, sacrificing to it and crying out, "These are your gods, Israel, who brought you up from the land of Egypt!" [9] I have seen this people, how stiff-necked they are, continued the LORD to Moses. [10] Let me alone, then, that my anger may burn against them to consume them. Then I will make of you a great nation.

[11] But Moses implored the LORD, his God, saying, "Why, O LORD, should your anger burn against your people, whom you brought out of the land of Egypt with great power and with a strong hand? [12] Why should the Egyptians say, 'With evil intent he brought them out, that he

continue

32:1-29 The Golden Calf

After having spent many chapters of the narrative on the heights of Mount Sinai, the account sets up a dramatic contrast between God's will for Israel as revealed to Moses and the real world of human frailty. On the mountain is revealed the ideal covenant characterized by harmony with God's will in moral action and proper worship. In the valley below is displayed a serious act of disloyalty that threatens to destroy the covenant itself and plunge Israel into a situation far more deadly than their bondage in Egypt. The forty days on the mountain, shown by the account as a time of extraordinary revelation, was interpreted by the people below as an intolerable delay.

Chapters 32–34 stand between the narrative of God's instructions for the tabernacle and Israel's obedience to those instructions (chaps. 35–40). The principal goal of the Exodus has been the freedom to worship YHWH. That freedom now leads to disaster as the detailed instructions for constructing the tabernacle are followed by the hasty erection of Israel's idol. The elaborate preparations required to protect the holiness of God's presence in the tabernacle are contrasted with the impulsive and seemingly overnight construction of an impersonal object. Aaron's demand for the golden earrings to create the idol is a sharp digression from the instructions to collect gold and materials from the willing hearts of the people (25:2). Aaron and the people of Israel foolishly sought immediate access to their invisible and dynamic God through a passive, tangible image. The foundational principle for relationship with YHWH, prohibition of the creation and worship of idols (20:4-5), had been violated.

Honoring the golden calf was not the worship of another god. It was an attempt to worship YHWH by a means that YHWH had already declared unacceptable. It was an attempt to represent God on Israel's terms—accessible, easily manipulated, passive, and confined. The proclamation, "These are your gods, Israel, who brought you up from the land of Egypt!" mocks the absolute freedom of YHWH who liberated Israel from bondage (v. 8). The fact that they built an altar and celebrated a sacred feast with sacrifices to YHWH indicates that their acts were outwardly religious but inwardly disloyal.

The form of the narrative has been influenced by countless instances of Israel's unfaithfulness throughout its history. The strongest influence is seen in King Jeroboam's later attempt to represent YHWH with golden calves at the shrines in Bethel and Dan (1 Kgs 12:28). While the temple of Jerusalem claimed the ark as a visible assurance of God's presence, Jeroboam wanted to set up a substitute symbol in the sanctuaries of the northern kingdom. The narrative in Exodus is told in a way that makes it representative of all subsequent idolatry on the part of Israel. As the tabernacle is a paradigm of all Israel's worship, the golden calf is a paradigm of all Israel's unfaithfulness and sin.

The strong contrast between what happens on the mountain and what transpires in the valley is continued in the various reactions of God and Moses to Israel's sin. On the mountain, God's judgment is immediate and unambiguous. God intends to annihilate the covenant and begin a new nation with Moses himself. Moses, however, pleads for God to reconsider. In the valley below, Moses' anger flares against Israel, while God is convinced to relent.

Moses intercedes for Israel and seeks to persuade God to relent with three arguments.

might kill them in the mountains and wipe them off the face of the earth'? Turn from your burning wrath; change your mind about punishing your people. [13]Remember your servants Abraham, Isaac, and Israel, and how you swore to them by your own self, saying, 'I will make your descendants as numerous as the stars in the sky; and all this land that I promised, I will give your descendants as their perpetual heritage.'" [14]So the LORD changed his mind about the punishment he had threatened to inflict on his people.

[15]Moses then turned and came down the mountain with the two tablets of the covenant in his hands, tablets that were written on both sides, front and back. [16]The tablets were made by God; the writing was the writing of God, engraved on the tablets. [17]Now, when Joshua heard the noise of the people shouting, he said to Moses, "That sounds like a battle in the camp." [18]But Moses answered,

"It is not the noise of victory,
    it is not the noise of defeat;
    the sound I hear is singing."

[19]As he drew near the camp, he saw the calf and the dancing. Then Moses' anger burned, and he threw the tablets down and broke them on the base of the mountain. [20]Taking the calf they had made, he burned it in the fire and then ground it down to powder, which he scattered on the water and made the Israelites drink.

[21]Moses asked Aaron, "What did this people do to you that you should lead them into a grave sin?" [22]Aaron replied, "Do not let my lord be angry. You know how the people are prone to evil. [23]They said to me, 'Make us a god to go before us; as for this man Moses who brought us out of the land of Egypt, we do not know what has happened to him.' [24]So I told them, 'Whoever is wearing gold, take it off.' They gave it to me, and I threw it into the fire, and this calf came out."

[25]Moses saw that the people were running wild because Aaron had lost control—to the secret delight of their foes. [26]Moses stood at the gate of

continue

the camp and shouted, "Whoever is for the LORD, come to me!" All the Levites then rallied to him, ²⁷and he told them, "Thus says the LORD, the God of Israel: Each of you put your sword on your hip! Go back and forth through the camp, from gate to gate, and kill your brothers, your friends, your neighbors!" ²⁸The Levites did as Moses had commanded, and that day about three thousand of the people fell. ²⁹Then Moses said, "Today you are installed as priests for the LORD, for you went against your own sons and brothers, to bring a blessing upon yourselves this day."

The Atonement

³⁰On the next day Moses said to the people, "You have committed a grave sin. Now I will go up to the LORD; perhaps I may be able to make atonement for your sin." ³¹So Moses returned to the LORD and said, "Ah, this people has committed a grave sin in making a god of gold for themselves! ³²Now if you would only forgive their sin! But if you will not, then blot me out of the book that you have written." ³³The LORD answered Moses: Only the one who has sinned against me will I blot out of my book. ³⁴Now, go and lead the

continue

First, he argues that YHWH has just liberated Israel from slavery and it would not be reasonable to reverse that action so soon. Second, he tells YHWH that it would give the Egyptians great satisfaction to see Israel destroyed and it would endanger YHWH's reputation among them. Third, he reminds YHWH about the divine promise of land and progeny made to the patriarchs. These persuasive arguments of Moses lead to the amazing reversal of God's intentions. The account demonstrates much about Israel's understanding of YHWH's nature. God's ability to be persuaded indicates that YHWH is not a static, unchanging being but rather the divine nature is personal, totally free, and responsive to the changing needs of a vital relationship with people.

Verse 15 narrates the descent of Moses to the people below. The suspense mounts as we wait for Moses' response. The uncompromising anger displayed by Moses when he saw the people's idolatry and revelry parallels the anger of YHWH on the mountain. Moses proceeds with an unbroken series of violent actions in which he demolishes both the tablets and the calf. The tablets symbolize the covenant, and the description that they were engraved by God on the front and back confirms that YHWH is the source and authority behind them. Smashing the tablets indicates that, from Moses' point of view, the covenant has been broken and terminated. The calf is utterly destroyed and made totally irretrievable as the people are made to ingest their own sin by drinking the ground remains.

Aaron seeks to dissipate Moses' anger by minimizing his own role and blaming it on the people. Aaron does not succeed with Moses as Moses had with God. Aaron accuses the people of being prone to evil while Moses had defended them before God's anger. Aaron divorces himself from responsibility by proclaiming that the calf came from the fire of its own accord while Moses took on the sin of the people to mediate their forgiveness.

Moses called Israel to make an uncompromising choice for or against YHWH: "Whoever is for the LORD, come to me!" (v. 26). The Levites who came forward became the agents of YHWH's judgment and displayed faithfulness even to the point of slaying their own kinsmen, family, and friends. They demonstrated the ability to provide Israel with religious leadership that would be loyal against all pressures to compromise the covenant. Israel's tradition assumed that such purging was required for the continuing life of the community. Such display of loyalty and zeal for true worship on the part of the Levites demonstrated that they should be the ministers of Israel's rituals.

32:30–33:6 The Atonement

The sin of the people and its consequences are the focus of these verses. In the Hebrew text, "sin" occurs eight times in verses 30-34.

The consequences of sin are inevitably harmful, and the future of Israel's relationship with God is put in serious jeopardy. Israel's sin creates a situation in which life and death hang in the balance.

Moses intercedes for the people in order to attain forgiveness of their sin, even offering his own life for the sake of the people's future. The "book" in which YHWH has inscribed those chosen to experience freedom and life is an image taken from the ancient practice of registering citizens. Being struck from YHWH's book expresses the natural consequences of sin, which is falling from God's favor, back into slavery and death. Chapter 32 ends by showing Israel exposed to the inevitable repercussions of sin.

Chapter 33 introduces even worse consequences of Israel's sin. While YHWH remains faithful to the promise of a future land and a messenger to guide them, God withdraws the divine intention to personally dwell in their midst. Since Israel built a golden calf instead of YHWH's tabernacle, they have seriously threatened their relationship with God. God's intention to dwell with them (25:8; 29:45) has been negated.

YHWH's decision, "I myself will not go up in your company," plunged the people of Israel into bitter grief. As a sign of their mourning, they took off their festive dress and any ornamentation. The people who were destined to be God's "treasured possession . . . a kingdom of priests, a holy nation" (19:5-6) are now called "a stiff-necked people" and threatened with extermination if YHWH should dwell too closely with them.

While Israel's future looks bleak, God has not closed off any possibilities. The narrative is opened to the next stage of God's dealing with Israel by the divine statement, "Let me think what to do with you." Moses will continue to intercede; God will continue to respond. YHWH is shown to be a God who is in genuine partnership with people, who remains open to the future. Israel realized that passively leaving the future in the hands of God alone is not what God desires. Through his intercession,

people where I have told you. See, my angel will go before you. When it is time for me to punish, I will punish them for their sin.

35Thus the LORD struck the people for making the calf, the one that Aaron made.

CHAPTER 33

1The LORD spoke to Moses: Go! You and the people whom you have brought up from the land of Egypt are to go up from here to the land about which I swore to Abraham, Isaac, and Jacob: I will give it to your descendants. 2Driving out the Canaanites, Amorites, Hittites, Perizzites, Hivites and Jebusites, I will send an angel before you 3to a land flowing with milk and honey. But I myself will not go up in your company, because you are a stiff-necked people; otherwise I might consume you on the way. 4When the people heard this painful news, they mourned, and no one wore any ornaments.

5The LORD spoke to Moses: Speak to the Israelites: You are a stiff-necked people. Were I to go up in your company even for a moment, I would destroy you. Now off with your ornaments! Let me think what to do with you. 6So, from Mount Horeb onward, the Israelites stripped off their ornaments.

continue

Moses helps shape a future that is different and better than if he had remained silent.

Following the paradigmatic pattern of creation, fall, and renewal, Israel has moved from her creation as a people to her fall into sin. Expelled from God's personal and abiding presence, Israel's future is now uncertain. The passage is transitional; it prepares the way for what God will do next as God continues to sort out the possibilities with Moses.

33:7-23 Moses' Intimacy with God

Though verses 7-11 are from a different tradition and clearly interrupt the narrative of

Moses' Intimacy with God

[7]Moses used to pitch a tent outside the camp at some distance. It was called the tent of meeting. Anyone who wished to consult the LORD would go to the tent of meeting outside the camp. [8]Whenever Moses went out to the tent, the people would all rise and stand at the entrance of their own tents, watching Moses until he entered the tent. [9]As Moses entered the tent, the column of cloud would come down and stand at its entrance while the LORD spoke with Moses. [10]On seeing the column of cloud stand at the entrance of the tent, all the people would rise and bow down at the entrance of their own tents. [11]The LORD used to speak to Moses face to face, as a person speaks to a friend. Moses would then return to the camp, but his young assistant, Joshua, son of Nun, never left the tent. [12]Moses said to the LORD, "See, you are telling me: Lead this people. But you have not let me know whom you will send with me. Yet you have said: You are my intimate friend; You have found favor with me. [13]Now, if I have found favor with you, please let me know your ways so that, in knowing you, I may continue to find favor with you. See, this nation

continue

faithful, it gives hope that Israel might continue that devotion in the future despite their failure. The editors use the passage to suspend the action for a while as Israel's fate hangs in the balance.

The "meeting tent" described here is a much older tradition than the tabernacle described in the Priestly tradition. It served as a place in which YHWH would periodically meet with Moses and reveal the divine will. It was at some distance outside the camp, whereas the tabernacle was to be placed in the midst of the people (25:8). The meeting tent was attended by Joshua, not by a family of priests; it was a place of periodic encounter, not a permanent dwelling for YHWH; it was a place exclusively for meeting with the divine, not a place for sacrifice and offerings. This earlier and simpler concept of Israel's meeting tent was later amalgamated with the Priestly tradition and replaced by the more elaborate tabernacle.

 The book of Exodus portrays Moses as God's "friend" (33:11-12, 17). This intimate way of characterizing a human-divine relationship is remarkable. Elsewhere in Scripture, Abraham is also called a **friend of God** (2 Chron 20:7; Isa 41:8). But this privileged relationship is not only reserved for ancient biblical figures. Scripture attests to God's desire to be friends with human beings. Wisdom 7:14 reads, "For [Wisdom] is an unfailing treasure; those who gain this treasure win the friendship of God." And Jesus says to those who have committed themselves to him, "I have called you friends" (John 15:15).

Moses' intercession for sinful Israel, the passage has been edited into this position because it was such an important memory for Israel. The connection to the present narrative concerns the role of Moses as intercessor before God. The verses emphasize the intimate, "face to face" relationship between Moses and YHWH. Because Moses is so close to God, there is some hope for Israel's future in their dialogue. All may not be lost for their future as YHWH's people.

The passage also gives a retrospective view of how things used to be. Israel used to faithfully seek God's will in the meeting tent, worship God appropriately from their own tents, and look to Moses as their mediator with YHWH. By showing that the people were once

Here again we find hints that the passage does not just record historical memory but it also describes Israel's worship in every age either at the temple in Jerusalem or at other public shrines. The people would stand outside in prayer as the priest entered the sanctuary.

When they saw the cloud of smoke rising from the incense altar, they would prostrate themselves in worship, knowing that Yнwн was truly present among them. The liturgical ritual described here assures the people of Israel in every generation that their worship of Yнwн is a participation in that foundational experience of relationship with God in the desert.

The narrative of Moses' intercession for sinful Israel is picked up again in verse 12 after the retrospective interlude of verses 7-11. Moses pleads with God to restore the divine presence with every argument he can think of, and God responds favorably to his requests. First, Moses reminds God that, although he has been told to lead the people on from there, God has not told him how this is to be done. Reminiscent of Moses' first question to God at the burning bush (3:11), Moses suggests that he cannot accomplish God's mission alone. Moses then presses his pleas on the strength of his intimacy with God and the favor God has found in him. Given this special intimacy, Moses suggests that he should be told God's ways, that is, what God's intentions are in this matter. Moses then reminds God that "this people" is indeed "your own people."

To Moses' masterfully convincing plea, Yнwн responds with assurance that the divine presence would be with Moses along the way. Yet Moses continues his plea, almost as if he didn't hear God. The emotional intensity continues as Moses seeks to obtain from God further assurance, not only for himself, but for all the people of Israel. Moses reminds Yнwн that only the divine presence distinguishes Israel from all the peoples of the world. Finally, in verse 17, God concludes this brief but effective dialogue by affirming that Moses' arguments have been convincing and that the constant presence of Yнwн would be given to Israel as they leave Sinai.

Having won the assurance of God's presence, Moses asks for a personal experience of God's presence to demonstrate the reality of the divine promise. God grants Moses' request in a modified way. Since no one can look upon God and still live, God plans to grant Moses a

is indeed your own people. [14]The LORD answered: I myself will go along, to give you rest. [15]Moses replied, "If you are not going yourself, do not make us go up from here. [16]For how can it be known that I and your people have found favor with you, except by your going with us? Then we, your people and I, will be singled out from every other people on the surface of the earth." [17]The LORD said to Moses: This request, too, which you have made, I will carry out, because you have found favor with me and you are my intimate friend.

[18]Then Moses said, "Please let me see your glory!" [19]The LORD answered: I will make all my goodness pass before you, and I will proclaim my name, "LORD," before you; I who show favor to whom I will, I who grant mercy to whom I will. [20]But you cannot see my face, for no one can see me and live. [21]Here, continued the LORD, is a place near me where you shall station yourself on the rock. [22]When my glory passes I will set you in the cleft of the rock and will cover you with my hand until I have passed by. [23]Then I will remove my hand, so that you may see my back; but my face may not be seen.

continue

revelation of the divine presence not in terms of a visible appearance but in terms of God's attributes. Yнwн will reveal to Moses not how God looks but how God is. Yнwн will make the divine "goodness" pass by and will pronounce the divine name. The theophany will not be a tangible manifestation of God but a revelation of God's essential nature expressed in a proclamation of God's name and a recitation of God's character.

This personal, mystical experience granted to Moses is described in anthropomorphic terms. God's own "hand" is used to prevent Moses from seeing the divine "face." When God has passed by, God will take away the hand so that Moses will be able to see the "back" of God. The back represents the aspect

CHAPTER 34

Renewal of the Tablets

¹The LORD said to Moses: "Cut two stone tablets like the former, that I may write on them the words which were on the former tablets that you broke. ²Get ready for tomorrow morning, when you are to go up Mount Sinai and there present yourself to me on the top of the mountain. ³No one shall come up with you, and let no one even be seen on any part of the mountain; even the sheep and the cattle are not to graze in front of this mountain." ⁴Moses then cut two stone tablets like the former, and early the next morning he went up Mount Sinai as the LORD had commanded him, taking in his hand the two stone tablets.

⁵The LORD came down in a cloud and stood with him there and proclaimed the name, "LORD." ⁶So the LORD passed before him and proclaimed: The LORD, the LORD, a God gracious and merciful, slow to anger and abounding in love and fidelity, ⁷continuing his love for a thousand generations, and forgiving wickedness, rebellion, and sin; yet not declaring the guilty guiltless, but bringing punishment for their parents' wickedness on children and children's children to the third and fourth generation! ⁸Moses at once knelt and bowed down to the ground. ⁹Then he said, "If I find favor with you, Lord, please, Lord, come along in our company. This is indeed a stiff-necked people; yet pardon our wickedness and sins, and claim us as your own."

continue

and mercy to whomever God wishes. YHWH is a God who "passes by," a God who is made known by divine actions, a dynamic presence described through images of motion. YHWH is not like the other gods who could be captured or contained in some human dwelling, or that could be manifested in a visible image.

The passage expresses the unchanging nature of Israel's presentation of YHWH in cultic worship. Surrounding cultures represented their gods through unveiling images in their ceremonies. YHWH, however, was an invisible God who forbade Israel to represent the divine presence through images. The manifestation of YHWH in Israel's worship was always through word. The revelation of God was expressed through a proclamation of the nature of God and all that YHWH had done for Israel. God's people realized that the very name of YHWH was in itself a promise of freedom and life.

34:1-9 Renewal of the Tablets

God's directive to cut new stone tablets like the first ones expresses God's willingness to begin again the relationship that has been broken by Israel's infidelity. Once again Moses is instructed to make Mount Sinai a sanctified ground that no person or beast may approach except Moses (19:12). Again YHWH will descend onto the mountain in a cloud and give a new revelation of the divine name and the divine nature.

At the burning bush Moses had asked God how he is to know if God is really with him. In response, God revealed the enigmatic divine name YHWH, "I will be who I will be." In response to Moses' renewed request for assurance of divine presence, God passes before him and again calls out the divine name, twice this time. Who YHWH is has been demonstrated in the saving events of Israel's liberation from slavery, the deliverance at the sea, nourishment in the wilderness, and covenant on the mountain. Now, this same God of freedom and life speaks the divine name again, giving Moses assurance of God's personal presence in the continuing journey from the mountain and into the land of promise.

of God that Israel will continue to experience as God goes ahead of them and leads them on their journey. The imagery suggests that God's presence can only be partially and dimly grasped by human beings, even by one like Moses.

The personal name of God, as seen in 3:14, is an expression of the absolute freedom of God. It is further described here in verse 19 as expressing YHWH's free choice to grant favors

The description of the divine nature in verses 6-7 is part of an ancient profession of faith. It contains some of Israel's oldest understanding of who Yhwh is as it was expressed in liturgical ritual. The five phrases describing the nature of Yhwh express the implications of the divine name. Through her saving history, Israel had come to know Yhwh as gracious, merciful, faithful, forgiving, and just. Before such a God, Moses could only prostrate himself in worship, acknowledge the sins of Israel, and implore Yhwh again for a sharing in the divine presence for all Israel.

34:10-26 Religious Laws

Just as the foundational covenant had been based on Yhwh's wondrous deliverance of Israel from slavery into freedom, the renewed covenant is grounded in an experience just as marvelous. Yhwh had delivered Israel from the self-imposed bondage of deadly sin and, through divine forgiveness, brought her back to the freedom and life that God's presence provides. God promises to work awe-inspiring "marvels" among the people of Israel. On her part, Israel must maintain exclusive loyalty in her worship of Yhwh.

The marvels that God will work concern the events associated with Israel's inheritance of the Promised Land. God will drive out those occupying the land of Canaan when the Israelites enter the land. Israel must not enter into any covenant relationships with these peoples and must remove all the cultic objects associated with Canaanite worship. The sin with the golden calf remains the archetypal sin of Israel, representing the constant temptation to religious compromise and syncretism.

The laws enumerated here contain elements that parallel both the Decalogue (chap. 20) and the Book of the Covenant (chaps. 21–23). The foundational commands are similar to those of the Ten Commandments: the prohibitions against having other gods and creating images of the divine (20:3-4). Here the expansions on the commands are related to the specific temptations that will face Israel in the new land. To the command to worship Yhwh alone is added

Religious Laws

10The LORD said: Here is the covenant I will make. Before all your people I will perform marvels never before done in any nation anywhere on earth, so that all the people among whom you live may see the work of the LORD. Awe-inspiring are the deeds I will perform with you! 11As for you, observe what I am commanding you today.

See, I am about to drive out before you the Amorites, Canaanites, Hittites, Perizzites, Hivites and Jebusites. 12Take care not to make a covenant with the inhabitants of the land that you are to enter; lest they become a snare among you. 13Tear down their altars; smash their sacred stones, and cut down their asherahs. 14You shall not bow down to any other god, for the LORD—"Jealous" his name—is a jealous God. 15Do not make a covenant with the inhabitants of the land; else, when they prostitute themselves with their gods and sacrifice to them, one of them may invite you and you may partake of the sacrifice. 16And when you take their daughters as wives for your sons, and their daughters prostitute themselves with their gods, they will make your sons do the same.

17You shall not make for yourselves molten gods.

18You shall keep the festival of Unleavened Bread. For seven days at the appointed time in the month of Abib you are to eat unleavened bread, as I commanded you; for in the month of Abib you came out of Egypt.

19To me belongs every male that opens the womb among all your livestock, whether in the herd or in the flock. 20The firstling of a donkey you shall redeem with a lamb; if you do not redeem it, you must break its neck. The firstborn among your sons you shall redeem.

No one shall appear before me empty-handed. 21Six days you may labor, but on the seventh day you shall rest; even during the seasons of plowing and harvesting you must rest.

22You shall keep the feast of Weeks with the first fruits of the wheat harvest, likewise, the feast

continue

of the Ingathering at the close of the year. ²³Three times a year all your men shall appear before the Lord, the LORD God of Israel. ²⁴Since I will drive out the nations before you and enlarge your territory, no one will covet your land when you go up three times a year to appear before the LORD, your God.

²⁵You shall not offer me the blood of sacrifice with anything leavened, nor shall the sacrifice of the Passover feast be kept overnight for the next day.

²⁶The choicest first fruits of your soil you shall bring to the house of the LORD, your God.

You shall not boil a young goat in its mother's milk.

Radiance of Moses' Face

²⁷Then the LORD said to Moses: Write down these words, for in accordance with these words I have made a covenant with you and with Israel. ²⁸So Moses was there with the LORD for forty days and forty nights, without eating any food or drinking any water, and he wrote on the tablets the words of the covenant, the ten words. ²⁹As Moses came down from Mount Sinai with the two tablets of the covenant in his hands, he did not know that the skin of his face had

continue

the prohibition against alliances or intermarriage with other peoples. The ban on making images specifically forbids the casting of molten idols, a direct reaction to Israel's sin with the golden calf. As in the Book of the Covenant, we see how the implications are drawn from the general principles according to the challenges of particular historical circumstances.

The remaining laws present a broad summary of some of the most important obligations of the covenant. Emphasis is on those laws that set Israel apart from other peoples and those that deal with right worship. The laws previously given are still valid, though these newly stated laws need particular em-

phasis in view of the challenges that will face Israel in relationship to their "jealous" God.

34:27-35 Radiance of Moses' Face

"These words" that God commands Moses to write down refer to all the words YHWH had spoken: promises, admonitions, and laws. Immediately after this command, we are told that Moses remained on the mountain with God for a long period of time; "forty days and forty nights" generally refers to a period of extraordinary revelation. It is not clear from the phrase whether it was Moses or YHWH who then wrote on the tablets "the words of the covenant, the ten words." However, the context implies that YHWH wrote the Ten Commandments to replace the tablets that had been broken. The phrase forms an inclusion with 34:1 and concludes the promise that YHWH had made at the beginning of the narrative. Thus, what YHWH wrote, the unchanging principles of the covenant, is distinguished from what Moses wrote, the historically modified ordinances that apply the unchanging law to the challenges of particular times and settings.

The reference to Moses' forty days and forty nights on Mount Sinai with the LORD (34:28) is one of many biblical references to **the number forty**, the most important being Israel's forty years of wandering in the desert before entering the land of Canaan (16:35). Forty years represents a generation or a complete cycle. Other biblical references include forty days and nights of flooding rain in Genesis (7:12), King David's forty year reign (2 Sam 5:4), and Jesus' forty day temptation in the desert (Mark 1:13).

The narrative of Israel's sin and renewal (chaps. 32–34) concludes with Moses' descent from Mount Sinai. The emphasis is on reestablishing Moses' authority as YHWH's representative in the eyes of the people, since that authority had been discredited through the people's sin. Moses' first descent had been met with rejection and rebellion (32:15ff.); his present descent is met with reverence and awe.

— Moses' radiant face after being in YHWH's presence expresses the authority he receives from God. The verb translated here as "become radiant" has been the source of much confusion since it is related to the Hebrew word meaning "horn." Thus older translations often misunderstood the text to imply that Moses had horns extending from his head (as seen in the art of Michelangelo and Chagall). A more literal translation would be "put out horn-like rays." The image suggests Moses having rays of light coming from his face. It is described as a shining that Moses was not aware of, a gift of God to Moses to reestablish his authority before the people.

Whenever Moses communicated with God, whether on Sinai, in the meeting tent or the tabernacle, and whenever Moses communicated God's words to the people, his face radiated as an afterglow from the immediate presence of God. Once more God has provided Moses with a sign for the people, a sign that Moses could not provide for himself. The sign leaves no doubt about the divine source of the words Moses communicates to the people. Moses related to the people "all that the LORD had told him on Mount Sinai" and Moses would continue to relate all that God communicated with him. Only after speaking God's word did Moses place the veil over his face to indicate that he was no longer speaking in God's name.

35:1-3 Sabbath Regulations

Chapters 35–40 detail how the commands given to Moses in chapters 25–31 were carried out. The two sections complement one another as instruction and obedience. It is obvious that much of the wording of the previous chapters is repeated here, often verbatim. This repetition is characteristic of the Priestly tradition and is intended to emphasize to Israel and its priests the importance of maintaining these symbols and liturgical practices as essential for its tradition.

become radiant while he spoke with the LORD. [30]When Aaron, then, and the other Israelites saw Moses and noticed how radiant the skin of his face had become, they were afraid to come near him. [31]Only after Moses called to them did Aaron and all the leaders of the community come back to him. Moses then spoke to them. [32]Later, all the Israelites came up to him, and he enjoined on them all that the LORD had told him on Mount Sinai. [33]When Moses finished speaking with them, he put a veil over his face. [34]Whenever Moses entered the presence of the LORD to speak with him, he removed the veil until he came out again. On coming out, he would tell the Israelites all that he had been commanded. [35]Then the Israelites would see that the skin of Moses' face was radiant; so he would again put the veil over his face until he went in to speak with the LORD.

VIII. The Building of the Tabernacle and the Descent of God's Glory upon It

CHAPTER 35

Sabbath Regulations

[1]Moses assembled the whole Israelite community and said to them, "These are the words the LORD has commanded to be observed. [2]On six days work may be done, but the seventh day shall be holy to you as the sabbath of complete rest to the LORD. Anyone who does work on that day shall be put to death. [3]You shall not even light a fire in any of your dwellings on the sabbath day."

continue

This final section of Exodus demonstrates how God's promise to dwell with Israel is fulfilled. Despite Israel's sin, God's promises allow Israel to build the tabernacle in anticipation of God's coming to dwell among them. In light of the period of exile in which the Priestly tradition was edited, Israel is assured again that just as God went forward with plans for a sanctuary after Israel's sin in the past, so God would again dwell with Israel in a renewed temple.

Collection of Materials

4Moses said to the whole Israelite community, "This is what the LORD has commanded: 5Receive from among you contributions for the LORD. Everyone, as his heart prompts him, shall bring, as a contribution to the LORD, gold, silver, and bronze; 6violet, purple, and scarlet yarn; fine linen and goat hair; 7rams' skins dyed red, and tahash skins; acacia wood; 8oil for the light; spices for the anointing oil and for the fragrant incense; 9onyx stones and other gems for mounting on the ephod and on the breastpiece.

Call for Artisans

10"Let every artisan among you come and make all that the LORD has commanded: 11the tabernacle, with its tent, its covering, its clasps, its frames, its bars, its columns, and its pedestals; 12the ark, with its poles, the cover, and the curtain veil; 13the table, with its poles and all its utensils, and the showbread; 14the menorah, with its utensils, the lamps, and the oil for the light; 15the altar of incense, with its poles; the anointing oil, and the fragrant incense; the entrance curtain for the entrance of the tabernacle; 16the altar for burnt offerings, with its bronze grating, its poles, and all its utensils; the basin, with its stand; 17the hangings of the court, with their columns and pedestals; the curtain for the gate of the court; 18the tent pegs for the tabernacle and for the court, with their ropes; 19the service cloths for use in the sanctuary; the sacred vestments for Aaron, the priest, and the vestments for his sons in their ministry."

The Contribution

20When the whole Israelite community left Moses' presence, 21all, as their hearts moved them and their spirit prompted, brought a contribution to the LORD for the work of the tent of meeting, for all its services, and for the sacred vestments. 22Both the men and the women, all as their heart prompted them, brought brooches, earrings, rings, necklaces, and various other gold articles. Everyone who could presented an offering of gold to the LORD. 23Everyone who happened to have violet, purple, or scarlet yarn, fine linen or goat hair, rams' skins dyed red or tahash skins, brought them. 24Whoever could make a contribution of silver or bronze offered it to the LORD; and everyone who happened to have acacia wood for any part of the work, brought it. 25All the women who were expert spinners brought hand-spun violet, purple, and scarlet yarn and fine linen thread. 26All the women, as their hearts and skills moved them, spun goat hair. 27The tribal leaders brought onyx stones and other gems for mounting on the ephod and on the breastpiece; 28as well as spices, and oil for the light, anointing oil, and fragrant incense. 29Every Israelite man and woman brought to the LORD such voluntary offerings as they thought best, for the various kinds of work which the LORD, through Moses, had commanded to be done.

The Artisans

30Moses said to the Israelites: "See, the LORD has singled out Bezalel, son of Uri, son of Hur, of the tribe of Judah, 31and has filled him with a divine spirit of skill and understanding and knowledge in every craft: 32in the production of embroidery, in making things of gold, silver, or bronze, 33in cutting and mounting precious stones, in carving wood, and in every other craft. 34He has also given both him and Oholiab, son of Ahisamach, of the tribe of Dan, the ability to teach others. 35He has endowed them with skill to execute all types of work: engraving, embroidering, the making of variegated cloth of violet, purple, and scarlet yarn and fine linen thread, weaving, and all other arts and crafts.

CHAPTER 36

1"Bezalel, therefore, will set to work with Oholiab and with all the artisans whom the LORD has endowed with skill and understanding in knowing how to do all the work for the service of the sanctuary, just as the LORD has commanded."

2Moses then called Bezalel and Oholiab and all the other artisans whom the LORD had en-

continue

This section begins where the earlier instructions on the mountain ended—with an emphasis on the Sabbath. This unique sign expressing Israel's God-given freedom and life forms a bridge, linking chapters 25–31 and chapters 35–40 together. The rhythm of work and leisure established for God's liberated people was especially important as Israel created its tabernacle for Yhwh.

35:4-9 Collection of Materials

Moses' call for the collection is a review of materials listed earlier to be brought by the people for the construction of the tabernacle. Repeated emphasis is given to the fact that the offering is voluntary. Obedience to the commands of Yhwh is internally motivated, not just an external compliance.

35:10-19 Call for Artisans

In addition to the call for material, there is a call for talent. The invitation to every skilled worker is not found in the previous instructions. Again, an inventory is given, which serves as a preview of all that is to be crafted.

35:20-29 The Contribution

The free-will offering includes not only the giving of materials but also voluntary skilled work. For the first time, particular mention is made of women, both for their contribution of personal jewelry and for their skilled spinning of cloth.

35:30–36:7 The Artisans

The overseers, Bezalel and Oholiab, have been given not only the skill to do all the work necessary for creating the sanctuary but also the ability to teach those skills to others. All those whose hearts were moved to join in the work were given the ability to fulfill all the necessary tasks.

The response of the people in bringing their voluntary offerings was so exuberant that Moses had to decree that no further contributions were to be made. The text encourages future generations to respond as zealously to Israel's communal worship.

dowed with skill, men whose hearts moved them to come and do the work. [3]They received from Moses all the contributions that the Israelites had brought for the work to be done for the sanctuary service. Still, morning after morning the people continued to bring their voluntary offerings to Moses. [4]Thereupon all the artisans who were doing the work for the sanctuary came from the work each was doing, [5]and told Moses, "The people are bringing much more than is needed to carry out the work which the LORD has commanded us to do." [6]Moses, therefore, ordered a proclamation to be made throughout the camp: "Let neither man nor woman make any more contributions for the sanctuary." So the people stopped bringing their offerings; [7]there was already enough at hand, and more than enough, to complete the work to be done.

The Tent Cloth and Coverings

[8]The various artisans who were doing the work made the tabernacle with its ten sheets woven of fine linen twined, having cherubim embroidered on them with violet, purple, and scarlet yarn. [9]The length of each sheet was twenty-eight cubits, and the width four cubits; all the sheets were the same size. [10]Five of the sheets were joined together, edge to edge; and the other five sheets likewise, edge to edge. [11]Loops of violet yarn were made along the edge of the end sheet in the first set, and the same along the edge of the end sheet in the second set. [12]Fifty loops were thus put on one inner sheet, and fifty loops on the inner sheet in the other set, with the loops directly opposite each other. [13]Then fifty clasps of gold were made, with

continue

36:8–38:20 Construction of the Ark

The order of construction follows a logical sequence, moving from the outer walls and frame of the tabernacle to its inner furnishings. These sections duplicate the earlier instructions with a few minor omissions.

The construction of the ark, table, menorah, and altar of incense are described in sequence which the sheets were joined so that the tabernacle formed one whole.

[14]Sheets of goat hair were also woven as a tent over the tabernacle. Eleven such sheets were made. [15]The length of each sheet was thirty cubits and the width four cubits; all eleven sheets were the same size. [16]Five of these sheets were joined into one set, and the other six sheets into another set. [17]Fifty loops were made along the edge of the end sheet in one set, and fifty loops along the edge of the corresponding sheet in the other set. [18]Fifty bronze clasps were made with which the tent was joined so that it formed one whole. [19]A covering for the tent was made of rams' skins dyed red and, above that, a covering of tahash skins.

The Framework

[20]Frames were made for the tabernacle, acaciawood uprights. [21]The length of each frame was ten cubits, and the width one and a half cubits. [22]Each frame had two arms, fastening them one to another. In this way all the frames of the tabernacle were made. [23]The frames for the tabernacle were made as follows: twenty frames on the south side, [24]with forty silver pedestals under the twenty frames, two pedestals under each frame for its two arms; [25]twenty frames on the other side of the tabernacle, the north side, [26]with their forty silver pedestals, two pedestals under each frame. [27]At the rear of the tabernacle, to the west, six frames were made, [28]and two frames were made for the corners of the tabernacle, at its rear. [29]These were double at the bottom, and likewise double at the top, to the first ring. That is how both corner frames were made. [30]Thus, there were eight frames, with their sixteen silver pedestals, two pedestals under each frame. [31]Bars of acacia wood were also made, five for the frames on one side of the tabernacle, [32]five for those on the other side, and five for those at the rear, to the west. [33]The center bar, at the middle of the frames, was made to reach across from end to end. [34]The frames were plated with gold, and gold rings were made on them as holders for the bars, which were also plated with gold.

The Veil

[35]The veil was made of violet, purple, and scarlet yarn, and of fine linen twined, with cherubim embroidered on it. [36]Four gold-plated columns of acacia wood, with gold hooks, were made for it, and four silver pedestals were cast for them.

[37]The curtain for the entrance of the tent was made of violet, purple, and scarlet yarn, and of fine linen twined, woven in a variegated manner. [38]Its five columns, with their hooks as well as their capitals and bands, were plated with gold; their five pedestals were of bronze.

CHAPTER 37

The Ark

[1]Bezalel made the ark of acacia wood, two and a half cubits long, one and a half cubits wide, and one and a half cubits high. [2]The inside and outside were plated with gold, and a molding of gold was put around it. [3]Four gold rings were cast for its four supports, two rings on one side and two on the opposite side. [4]Poles of acacia wood were made and plated with gold; [5]these poles were put through the rings on the sides of the ark, for carrying it.

[6]The cover was made of pure gold, two and a half cubits long and one and a half cubits wide. [7]Two cherubim of beaten gold were made for the two ends of the cover; [8]one cherub was at one end, the other at the other end, made of one piece with the cover, at each end. [9]The cherubim had their wings spread out above, sheltering the cover. They faced each other, with their faces looking toward the cover.

The Table

[10]The table was made of acacia wood, two cubits long, a cubit wide, and a cubit and a half high. [11]It was plated with pure gold, and a molding of gold was put around it. [12]A frame a handbreadth high was also put around it, with a molding of gold around the frame. [13]Four rings of gold were

continue

cast for it and fastened at the four corners, one at each leg. [14]The rings were alongside the frame as holders for the poles to carry the table. [15]These poles for carrying the table were made of acacia wood and plated with gold. [16]The vessels that were set on the table, its plates and cups, as well as its pitchers and bowls for pouring libations, were made of pure gold.

The Menorah

[17]The menorah was made of pure beaten gold—its shaft and branches—with its cups and knobs and petals springing directly from it. [18]Six branches extended from its sides, three branches on one side and three on the other. [19]On one branch there were three cups, shaped like almond blossoms, each with its knob and petals; on the opposite branch there were three cups, shaped like almond blossoms, each with its knob and petals; and so for the six branches that extended from the menorah. [20]On the menorah there were four cups, shaped like almond blossoms, with their knobs and petals. [21]The six branches that went out from the menorah had a knob under each pair. [22]The knobs and branches so sprang from it that the whole formed but a single piece of pure beaten gold. [23]Its seven lamps, as well as its trimming shears and trays, were made of pure gold. [24]A talent of pure gold was used for the menorah and its various utensils.

The Altar of Incense

[25]The altar of incense was made of acacia wood, on a square, a cubit long, a cubit wide, and two cubits high, having horns that sprang directly from it. [26]Its grate on top, its walls on all four sides, and its horns were plated with pure gold; and a gold molding was put around it. [27]Underneath the molding gold rings were placed, two on one side and two on the opposite side, as holders for the poles used in carrying it. [28]The poles, too, were made of acacia wood and plated with gold.

[29]The sacred anointing oil and the fragrant incense were prepared in their pure form by a perfumer.

CHAPTER 38

The Altar for Burnt Offerings

[1]The altar for burnt offerings was made of acacia wood, on a square, five cubits long and five cubits wide; its height was three cubits. [2]At the four corners horns were made that sprang directly from the altar. It was then plated with bronze. [3]All the utensils of the altar, the pots, shovels, basins, forks and fire pans, were likewise made of bronze. [4]A grating, a bronze network, was made for the altar and placed around it, on the ground, half as high as the altar itself. [5]Four rings were cast for the four corners of the bronze grating, as holders for the poles, [6]which were made of acacia wood and plated with bronze. [7]The poles were put through the rings on the sides of the altar for carrying it. The altar was made in the form of a hollow box.

[8]The bronze basin, with its bronze stand, was made from the mirrors of the women who served at the entrance of the tent of meeting.

continue

because they are all articles of worship for the holy place and the holy of holies. There is no new information added, though some details not related to the construction have been omitted.

Following the construction of the inner parts of the tabernacle, the construction of the altar for burnt offering, the bronze basin, and the courtyard in which they are to be placed is narrated. The new note concerns the construction of the basin from the bronze mirrors of "the women who served at the entrance of the tent of meeting." The verb suggests some form of organized ministerial service performed by these women.

The Court of the Tabernacle

⁹The court was made as follows. On the south side the hangings of the court were of fine linen twined, a hundred cubits long, ¹⁰with twenty columns and twenty pedestals of bronze, the hooks and bands of the columns being of silver. ¹¹On the north side there were similar hangings, a hundred cubits long, with twenty columns and twenty pedestals of bronze; the hooks and bands of the columns were of silver. ¹²On the west side there were hangings, fifty cubits long, with ten columns and ten pedestals; the hooks and bands of the columns were of silver. ¹³On the east side the court was fifty cubits. ¹⁴On one side there were hangings to the extent of fifteen cubits, with three columns and three pedestals; ¹⁵on the other side, beyond the gate of the court, there were likewise hangings to the extent of fifteen cubits, with three columns and three pedestals. ¹⁶The hangings on all sides of the court were woven of fine linen twined. ¹⁷The pedestals of the columns were of bronze, while the hooks and bands of the columns were of silver; the capitals were silver-plated, and all the columns of the court were banded with silver.

¹⁸At the gate of the court there was a variegated curtain, woven of violet, purple, and scarlet yarn and of fine linen twined, twenty cubits long and five cubits wide, in keeping with the hangings of the court. ¹⁹There were four columns and four pedestals of bronze for it, while their hooks were of silver, and their capitals and their bands silver-plated. ²⁰All the tent pegs for the tabernacle and for the court around it were of bronze.

Amount of Metal Used

²¹The following is an account of the various amounts used on the tabernacle, the tabernacle of the covenant, drawn up at the command of Moses by the Levites under the direction of Ithamar, son of Aaron the priest. ²²However, it was Bezalel, son of Uri, son of Hur, of the tribe of Judah, who made all that the LORD commanded Moses, ²³and he was assisted by Oholiab, son of Ahisamach, of the tribe of Dan, who was an engraver, an embroi- derer, and a weaver of variegated cloth of violet, purple, and scarlet yarn and of fine linen.

²⁴All the gold used in the entire construction of the sanctuary, having previously been given as an offering, amounted to twenty-nine talents and seven hundred and thirty shekels, according to the standard of the sanctuary shekel. ²⁵The silver of those of the community who were enrolled was one hundred talents and one thousand seven hundred and seventy-five shekels, according to the standard of the sanctuary shekel; ²⁶one bekah apiece, that is, a half-shekel, according to the standard of the sanctuary shekel, was received from everyone who was enrolled, of twenty years or more, namely, six hundred and three thousand five hundred and fifty men. ²⁷One hundred talents of silver were used for casting the pedestals of the sanctuary and the pedestals of the veil, one talent for each pedestal, or one hundred talents for the one hundred pedestals. ²⁸The remaining one thousand seven hundred and seventy-five shekels were used for making the hooks on the columns, for plating the capitals, and for banding them with silver. ²⁹The bronze, given as an offering, amounted to seventy talents and two thousand four hundred shekels. ³⁰With this were made the pedestals at the entrance of the tent of meeting, the bronze altar with its bronze gratings, and all the utensils of the altar, ³¹the pedestals around the court, the pedestals at the gate of the court, and all the tent pegs for the tabernacle and for the court around it.

CHAPTER 39

The Priestly Vestments

¹With violet, purple, and scarlet yarn were woven the service cloths for use in the sanctuary, as well as the sacred vestments for Aaron, as the LORD had commanded Moses.

²The ephod was woven of gold thread and of violet, purple, and scarlet yarn and of fine linen twined. ³Gold was first hammered into gold leaf and then cut up into threads, which were woven

continue

with the violet, purple, and scarlet yarn into an embroidered pattern on the fine linen. [4]Shoulder straps were made for it and joined to its two upper ends. [5]The embroidered belt on the ephod extended out from it, and like it, was made of gold thread, of violet, purple, and scarlet yarn, and of fine linen twined, as the LORD had commanded Moses. [6]The onyx stones were prepared and mounted in gold filigree work; they were engraved like seal engravings with the names of the sons of Israel. [7]These stones were set on the shoulder straps of the ephod as memorial stones of the sons of Israel, just as the LORD had commanded Moses.

[8]The breastpiece was embroidered like the ephod, with gold thread and violet, purple, and scarlet yarn on cloth of fine linen twined. [9]It was square and folded double, a span high and a span wide in its folded form. [10]Four rows of precious stones were mounted on it: in the first row a carnelian, a topaz, and an emerald; [11]in the second row, a garnet, a sapphire, and a beryl; [12]in the third row a jacinth, an agate, and an amethyst; [13]in the fourth row a chrysolite, an onyx, and a jasper. They were mounted in gold filigree work. [14]These stones were twelve, to match the names of the sons of Israel, and each stone was engraved like a seal with the name of one of the twelve tribes.

[15]Chains of pure gold, twisted like cords, were made for the breastpiece, [16]together with two gold filigree rosettes and two gold rings. The two rings were fastened to the two upper ends of the breastpiece. [17]The two gold chains were then fastened to the two rings at the ends of the breastpiece. [18]The other two ends of the two chains were fastened in front to the two filigree rosettes, which were attached to the shoulder straps of the ephod. [19]Two other gold rings were made and put on the two lower ends of the breastpiece, on the edge facing the ephod. [20]Two more gold rings were made and fastened to the bottom of the two shoulder straps next to where they joined the ephod in front, just above its embroidered belt. [21]Violet ribbons bound the rings of the breastpiece to the rings of the ephod, so that the breastpiece stayed right above the embroidered belt of the ephod and did not swing loose from it. All this was just as the LORD had commanded Moses.

Other Vestments

[22]The robe of the ephod was woven entirely of violet yarn, [23]with an opening in its center like the opening of a shirt, with selvage around the opening to keep it from being torn. [24]At the hem of the robe pomegranates were made of violet, purple, and scarlet yarn and of fine linen twined; [25]bells of pure gold were also made and put

continue

38:21-31 Amount of Metal Used

The amount of gold, silver, and bronze used in the construction of the sanctuary and its court, a summary of the voluntary offerings of the people, is itemized. Its listing serves to underscore again the unreserved generosity of the people and to testify to the magnificence of the place built for YHWH's dwelling. The amount of these metals is indeed remarkable, though not at all unrealistic for Israel's later temple in Jerusalem. Such abundance was not unusual for divine and royal structures in the ancient Near East. The Priestly tradition considered such opulence as entirely appropriate for the worship of YHWH's presence among them.

39:1-31 The Vestments

The text continually emphasizes how the divine instructions given on the mountain were carried out in precise detail. Verses 1, 5, 7, 21, 26, 29, and 31 repeat the phrase, "as the LORD had commanded Moses." The text emphasizes the divine origin and authority of the cultic vestments as commanded through Moses and the precision with which YHWH's instructions are to be carried out.

between the pomegranates all around the hem of the robe: [26]a bell, a pomegranate, a bell, a pomegranate, all around the hem of the robe which was to be worn in performing the ministry—all this, just as the LORD had commanded Moses.

[27]For Aaron and his sons there were also woven tunics of fine linen; [28]the turban of fine linen; the ornate skullcaps of fine linen; linen pants of fine linen twined; [29]and sashes of variegated work made of fine linen twined and of violet, purple, and scarlet yarn, as the LORD had commanded Moses. [30]The plate of the sacred diadem was made of pure gold and inscribed, as on a seal engraving: "Sacred to the LORD." [31]It was tied over the turban with a violet ribbon, as the LORD had commanded Moses.

Presentation of the Work to Moses

[32]Thus the entire work of the tabernacle of the tent of meeting was completed. The Israelites did the work just as the LORD had commanded Moses; so it was done. [33]They then brought to Moses the tabernacle, the tent with all its furnishings, the clasps, the frames, the bars, the columns, the pedestals, [34]the covering of rams' skins dyed red, the covering of tahash skins, the curtain veil; [35]the ark of the covenant with its poles, the cover, [36]the table with all its utensils and the showbread, [37]the pure gold menorah with its lamps set up on it and with all its utensils, the oil for the light, [38]the golden altar, the anointing oil, the fragrant incense; the curtain for the entrance of the tent, [39]the altar of bronze with its bronze grating, its poles and all its utensils, the basin with its stand, [40]the hangings of the court with their columns and pedestals, the curtain for the gate of the court with its ropes and tent pegs, all the equipment for the service of the tabernacle of the tent of meeting; [41]the service cloths for use in the sanctuary, the sacred vestments for Aaron the priest, and the vestments to be worn by his sons in their ministry. [42]Just as the LORD had commanded Moses, so the Israelites had carried out all the work. [43]So when Moses saw that all the work was done just as the LORD had commanded, he blessed them.

CHAPTER 40

Setting up the Tabernacle

[1]Then the LORD said to Moses: [2]On the first day of the first month you shall set up the tabernacle of the tent of meeting. [3]Put the ark of the covenant in it, and screen off the ark with the veil. [4]Bring in the table and set it. Then bring in the menorah and set up the lamps on it. [5]Put the golden altar of incense in front of the ark of the covenant, and hang the curtain at the entrance of the tabernacle. [6]Put the altar for burnt offerings in front of the entrance of the tabernacle of the tent of meeting. [7]Place the basin between the tent of meeting and the altar, and put water in it. [8]Set up the court round about, and put the curtain at the gate of the court.

[9]Take the anointing oil and anoint the tabernacle and everything in it, consecrating it and all its furnishings, so that it will be sacred. [10]Anoint the altar for burnt offerings and all its utensils, consecrating it, so that it will be most sacred. [11]Likewise, anoint the basin with its stand, and thus consecrate it.

[12]Then bring Aaron and his sons to the entrance of the tent of meeting, and there wash them with water. [13]Clothe Aaron with the sacred vestments and anoint him, thus consecrating him as my priest. [14]Bring forward his sons also, and clothe them with the tunics. [15]As you have anointed their father, anoint them also as my priests. Thus, by being anointed, shall they receive a perpetual priesthood throughout all future generations.

[16]Moses did just as the LORD had commanded him. [17]On the first day of the first month of the second year the tabernacle was set up. [18]It was Moses who set up the tabernacle. He placed its pedestals, set up its frames, put in its bars, and set up its columns. [19]He spread the tent over the tabernacle and put the covering on top of the tent, as the LORD had commanded him. [20]He took the covenant and put it in the ark; he placed poles alongside the ark and set the cover upon it. [21]He

continue

39:32-43 Presentation of the Work to Moses

When all the work was completed, everything that had been made was brought to Moses. The expansive inventory, drawn from the separate narratives of construction, fittingly closes and summarizes the account of the construction. Only Moses, who had received Yhwh's instructions on Sinai, was able to determine whether everything that had been made was in keeping with the divine intentions. After inspecting all the workmanship and finding that it had been completed "just as the Lord had commanded," Moses blessed them. Now all is ready for the erection and furnishing of the tabernacle and the anticipation of Yhwh's indwelling presence.

40:1-33 Setting up the Tabernacle

This synopsis of the sacred place, the sacred objects, and the sacred actions is joined to a sacred time, the first new moon of the year after the Exodus from Egypt. The climactic summary follows the two-part structure of the Priestly account. Yhwh's instructions to Moses for setting up the tabernacle (vv. 1-15) parallel the commands of chapters 25–31; Moses' obedience to God's instructions (vv. 16-33) parallel the obedience of Israel in chapters 35–40.

The prominent verbs of verses 9-15 are "anoint" and "consecrate." The focus of this section is not only the construction of the tabernacle but also its dedication as the sacramental means of divine presence with Israel. The sanctuary and all its furnishings, as well as Aaron and his sons, are to be anointed. The oil filled them with a vitality that was a share in the life of Yhwh. It set them apart for sacred purposes, and gave them a share in the holiness of God.

Again the text emphasizes that the divine instructions were carried out by Moses without variation. The formulaic expression "as the Lord had commanded him" appears as a refrain after Moses fulfills each command (vv. 16, 19, 21, 23, 25, 27, 29, 32). Finally Moses finished all the work he had been given to do (v. 33).

brought the ark into the tabernacle and hung the curtain veil, thus screening off the ark of the covenant, as the Lord had commanded him. [22]He put the table in the tent of meeting, on the north side of the tabernacle, outside the veil, [23]and arranged the bread on it before the Lord, as the Lord had commanded him. [24]He placed the menorah in the tent of meeting, opposite the table, on the south side of the tabernacle, [25]and he set up the lamps before the Lord, as the Lord had commanded him. [26]He placed the golden altar in the tent of meeting, in front of the veil, [27]and on it he burned fragrant incense, as the Lord had commanded him. [28]He hung the curtain at the entrance of the tabernacle. [29]He put the altar for burnt offerings in front of the entrance of the tabernacle of the tent of meeting, and sacrificed burnt offerings and grain offerings on it, as the Lord had commanded him. [30]He placed the basin between the tent of meeting and the altar, and put water in it for washing. [31]Moses and Aaron and his sons used to wash their hands and feet there, [32]for they washed themselves whenever they went into the tent of meeting or approached the altar, as the Lord had commanded Moses. [33]Finally, he set up the court around the tabernacle and the altar and hung curtain at the gate of the court.

Thus Moses finished all the work.

God's Presence in the Tabernacle

[34]Then the cloud covered the tent of meeting, and the glory of the Lord filled the tabernacle. [35]Moses could not enter the tent of meeting, because the cloud settled down upon it and the glory of the Lord filled the tabernacle. [36]Whenever the cloud rose from the tabernacle, the Israelites would set out on their journey. [37]But if the cloud did not lift, they would not go forward; only when it lifted did they go forward. [38]The cloud of the Lord was over the tabernacle by day, and fire in the cloud at night, in the sight of the whole house of Israel in all the stages of their journey.

40:34-38 God's Presence in the Tabernacle

The goal of the Priestly narrative of the tabernacle is reached—"that I may dwell in their midst" (25:8). When all was ready, God fulfilled the divine promise and came to dwell among the people of Israel. The conclusion of Exodus thus begins the corporate worship of YHWH by the people of Israel.

The "glory of YHWH," manifested on the mountain of Sinai in the descending cloud and fire, now fills the sanctuary. The presence of YHWH, experienced by Moses in the faraway heights, now draws near and dwells with God's people. Moses could not immediately enter the sanctuary because God's glory filled it. As on Sinai, he awaited God's further invitation to approach and enter into the divine presence.

The conclusion of Exodus also anticipates Israel's ongoing journey through the wilderness and the entry into the land of God's promise. YHWH is a God on the move, as unpredictable as the clouds, as unconstrained as fire. God's presence guides and protects the people of God as the journey continues.

Israel's foundational story, which had begun with the people's bondage to an unchanging system and to the oppressive presence of Pharaoh, now concludes with Israel in the service of the God who journeys with them, who cannot be held bound, who invites them to the ever-new challenges of freedom. God, who is the source and sustainer of all life, now dwells among the people to give them abundance of life on the journey to full life. As the story is retold in every generation, the people of God are called into covenant with the God of freedom and life. They are liberated and enlivened as the journey continues in every age.

 The narrative account of Israel's journey through the wilderness will continue in the book of **Numbers**, which recounts a thirty-eight year journey from Sinai to the promised land of Canaan. As the book of Numbers comes to an end, Israel is on the threshold of the promised land, awaiting entrance. The narrative continues in the book of **Joshua**. The divine promise of land is finally fulfilled as Israel, now led by Joshua as Moses' successor, enters Canaan and claims the land.

EXPLORING LESSON FOUR

1. a) Given what you know of salvation history, how does initial enthusiasm ("Everything the Lord has said, we will do," 19:8; 24:3) get tested over time (32:1-6)? (See Matt 13:20-21.)

We complain and rebel forgetting everything God has done. We mistakingly return toward the way of the world. We stray

b) What spiritual habits or disciplines can anchor us in faithfulness to God?

Regular prayer, Mass, Study of Scripture, spiritual reading, singing, spending time with other Christians.

2. Israel's disobedience of God's command leads to idolatry (32:4-8). Give some examples of idolatry in our culture today. (See Acts 7:39-41; Phil 3:18-20; Col 3:5.)

Politics, sports, fashion, status symbols, internet TV, money, statues, luxury

3. On what basis does Moses plead with God on behalf of those who are worshiping the image of a molten calf (32:11-14, 30-34)? (See Deut 9:25-29; Ps 106:23.)

Why turn against the people you brought out of Egypt? Why let the Egyptians say You had evil intent? Remember your servants Abraham, Isaac & Israel? I will make descendants as numerous as the stars

4. List some of the positive and negative examples of spiritual leadership found in Exodus 32.

Negative - Aaron was persuaded by the people to build a golden idol to worship rather than persuade & wait for Moses.
Positive - Moses intercedes for the people to ask for forgiveness from God

5. How might we reconcile God's wrath (32:10) with God's kindness and mercy (34:6-7)? (See Ps 103:8-13; Lam 3:22-23; Rom 2:5-8.)

_____

_____

_____

_____

_____

6. Within the book of Exodus, one tradition says that Moses spoke with God "face to face" (33:11) while another tradition says that Moses could not see the face of God and live (33:18-23). (See Num 12:7-8; Deut 34:10.) How do both traditions preserve ancient Israel's understanding of YHWH?

The radiance of Moses' face after being in the presence of God on Mt. Sinai

7. Israel preserved the description of God found in 34:6-7. Write your own description of God based on your understanding and experiences.

God above all gods, dwelling among his people, loving unconditionally, guiding with his Holy Spirit, forgiving our sins; offering us a continual relationship with Herself; considerate of our failings and frailties + weakness our only hope, calling us to Herself.

8. Why do chapters 35–40 repeat much of the information from chapters 25–31? (See 39:32.)

_____

_____

_____

_____

_____

9. After Moses has taken great care to set up the tabernacle in the tent of meeting, "the glory of the Lord filled the tabernacle" (40:34). As Catholic Christians, we may be reminded of God's presence with us in the Eucharist, in our own tabernacles. How does the Exodus account help you appreciate that God is both present with us in time and place, *and* completely infinite and unable to be contained?

_____

_____

_____

_____

_____

10. a) Every life is a story of Exodus. Where are you in the Exodus story? In need of liberation? Afraid to cross the waters into the unknown? Wandering in the desert? At the base of Mount Sinai? Awaiting entrance into Canaan?

The more we give to God, the more freedom we experience. There will always be a path on our personal journey, our own wandering in the deserts, experience and returning to the Lord, Covenant, rebellion, repentance, new beginnings

b) Share with your group your impressions of Exodus and what you enjoyed most about your group study experience.

_____

_____

_____

_____

CLOSING PRAYER

Prayer

*The cloud of the L*ORD *was over the tabernacle by day, and fire in the cloud at night, in the sight of the whole house of Israel in all the stages of their journey.* (Exod 40:38)

God of freedom and life, the sacred book of Exodus is a story of liberation, devotion, hardship, relationship, and love. As we incorporate this story into our own lives, help us to understand and to live the beauty of this book—the beauty of journey and covenant, of sin and forgiveness, of worship and divine presence. You free us, you forgive us, you teach us, you are with us. For this, we thank you.

And like ancient Israel, we come to you with generous hearts and with devotion to you, our one true God. We pray for one another and for all of those we hold in our hearts this day, especially . . .

PRAYING WITH YOUR GROUP

Because we know that the Bible allows us to hear God's voice, prayer provides the context for our study and sharing. By speaking and listening to God and each other, the discussion often grows to more deeply bond us to one another and to God.

At *the beginning and end of each lesson* simple prayers are provided for individual use, and also may be used within the group setting. Most of the closing prayers provided with each lesson relate directly to a theme from that lesson and encourage you to pray together for people and events in your local community.

Of course, there are many ways to center ourselves in God's presence as we gather together in groups around the word of God. We provide some additional suggestions here knowing you and your group will make prayer a priority as part of your gathering. These are simply alternative ways to pray if your group would like to try something different from those prayers provided in the previous pages.

Conversational Prayer

This form of prayer allows for the group members to pray in their own words in a way that is not intimidating. The group leader begins with Step One, inviting all to focus on the presence of Christ among them. After a few moments of quiet, the group leader invites anyone in the group to voice a prayer or two of thanksgiving; once that is complete, then anyone who has personal intentions may pray in their own words for their needs; finally, the group prays for the needs of others.

A suggested process:
In your own words, speak simple and short prayers to allow time for others to add their voices.

Focus on one "step" at a time, not worrying about praying for everything in your mental list at once.

Step One	Visualize Christ. Welcome him. Imagine him present with you in your group. Allow time for some silence.
Step Two	Gratitude opens our hearts. Use simple words such as, "Thank you, Lord, for . . ."
Step Three	Pray for your own needs knowing that others will pray with you. Be specific and honest. Use "I" and "me" language.

Step Four	Pray for others by name, with love.
	You may voice your agreement ("Yes, Lord").
	End with gratitude for sharing concerns.

Praying Like Ignatius

St. Ignatius Loyola, whose life and ministry are the foundation of the Jesuit community, invites us to enter into Scripture texts in order to experience the scenes, especially scenes of the gospels or other narrative parts of Scripture. Simply put, this is a method of creatively imagining the scene, viewing it from the inside, and asking God to meet you there. Most often, this is a personal form of prayer but in a group setting, some of its elements can be helpful if you allow time for this process.

A suggested process:

- Select a scene from the chapters in the particular lesson.
- Read that scene out loud in the group, followed by some quiet time.
- Ask group members to place themselves in the scene (as a character, or as an onlooker) so that they can imagine the emotions, responses, and thinking that may have taken place. Notice the details and the tone, and imagine the interaction with the Lord that is taking place.
- Share with the group any insights that came to you in this quiet imagining.
- Allow each person in the group to thank God for some insight and to pray about some request that may have surfaced.

Sacred Reading (or Lectio Divina)

This method of prayer invites us to "listen with the ear of the heart" as St. Benedict's rule would say. We listen to the words and the phrasing, asking God to speak to our innermost being. Again, this method of prayer is most often used in an individual setting but may also be used in an adapted way within a group.

A suggested process:

- Select a scene from the chapters in the particular lesson.
- Read the scene out loud in the group, perhaps two times.
- Ask group members to ponder a word or phrase that stands out to them.
- The group members could then simply speak the word or phrase as a kind of litany of what was meaningful for your group.
- Allow time for more silence to ponder the words that were heard, asking God to reveal to you what message you are meant to hear, how God is speaking to you.
- Follow up with spoken intentions at the close of this group time.

REFLECTING ON SCRIPTURE

Reading Scripture is an opportunity not simply to learn new information but to listen to God who loves you. Pray that the same Holy Spirit who guided the formation of Scripture will inspire you to correctly understand what you read, and empower you to make what you read a part of your life.

The inspired word of God contains layers of meaning. As you make your way through passages of Scripture, whether studying a book of the Bible or focusing on a biblical theme, you may find it helpful to ask yourself these four questions:

What does the Scripture passage say?
Read the passage slowly and reflectively. Become familiar with it. If the passage you are reading is a narrative, carefully observe the characters and the plot. Use your imagination to picture the scene or enter into it.

What does the Scripture passage mean?
Read the footnotes in your Bible and the commentary provided to help you understand what the sacred writers intended and what God wants to communicate by means of their words.

What does the Scripture passage mean to me?
Meditate on the passage. God's word is living and powerful. What is God saying to you? How does the Scripture passage apply to your life today?

What am I going to do about it?
Try to discover how God may be challenging you in this passage. An encounter with God contains a challenge to know God's will and follow it more closely in daily life. Ask the Holy Spirit to inspire not only your mind but your life with this living word.

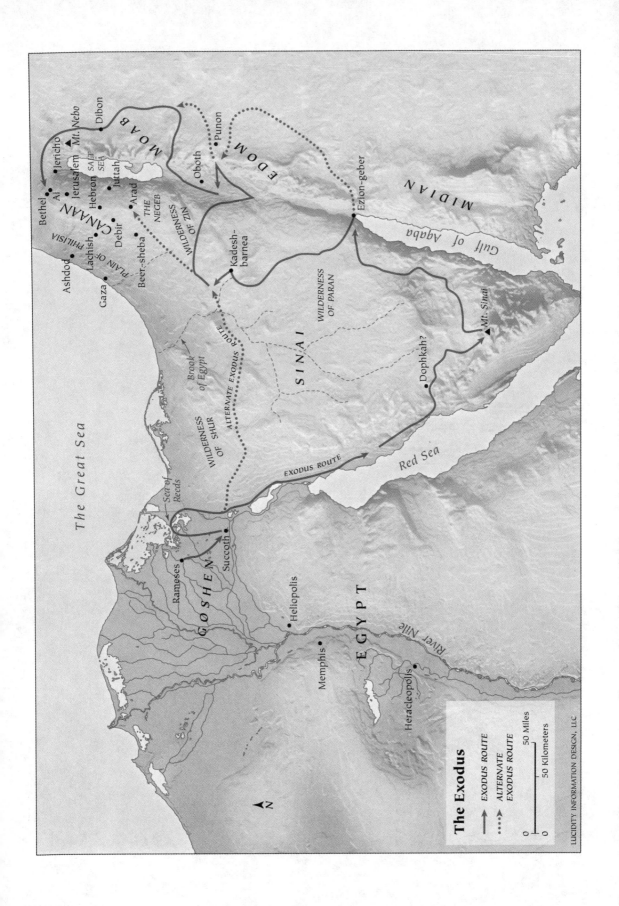

The Exodus

EXODUS ROUTE

ALTERNATE
EXODUS ROUTE

0   50 Miles

0   50 Kilometers

LUCIDITY INFORMATION DESIGN, LLC